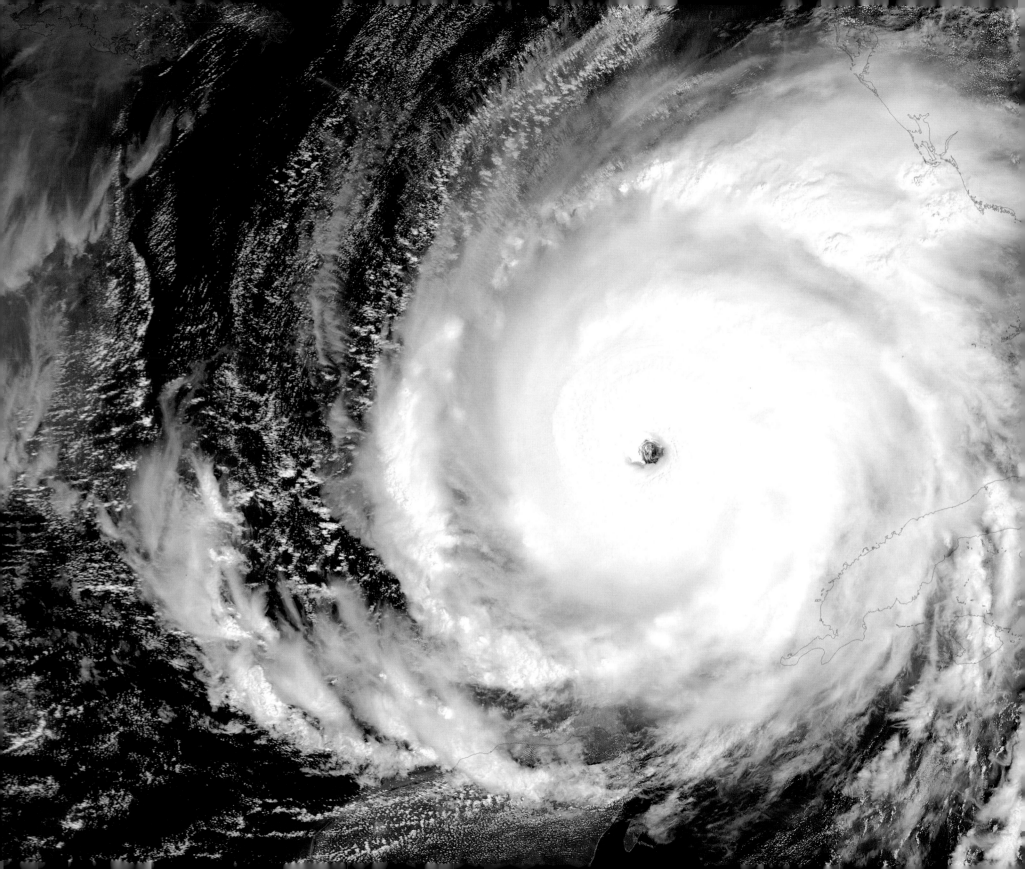

EYE OF THE STORM

NASA, Drones, and the Race to Crack the Hurricane Code

AMY CHERRIX

Houghton Mifflin Harcourt
Boston   New York

For Angela

The text of this book is set in Adobe Garamond Pro and Interstate

Library of Congress Cataloging-in-Publication Data
Names: Cherrix, Amy E., author
Title: Eye of the storm : NASA, drones, and the race to crack the hurricane code / by Amy Cherrix.
Description: Boston : Houghton Mifflin Harcourt, 2017.
Identifiers: LCCN 2016002792 | ISBN 9780544411654
Subjects: LCSH: Hurricanes. | Storm chasers. | Drone aircraft.
Classification: LCC QC944 .C45 2017 | DDC 551.55/2072—dc23
LC record available at https://lccn.loc.gov/2016002792

Printed in China
SCP 10 9 8 7 6 5 4 3 2 1
4500639499

PHOTO CREDITS:

Corbis: 4 (bottom), 5 (left), 56, 59; Jacques Descloitres, MODIS Rapid Response Team
at NASA GSFC: i; Angela Dresch: 1; FEMA: 7 (left), 61, 62; D. Fratello/NASA/AFRC: 50;
Getty Images: 4 (top), 57; Jenny Goldstick/HMH: 8, 35; Governing.com: 6 (sidebar photo);
Houghton Mifflin Harcourt: 58; Infographic World (www.InfographicWorld.com): 12; Norman
Kuring/NASA/Ocean Color Web: vi-1; Joseph Lamberti: ii-iii, iv-v, 14, 17 (left), 21, 22, 24,
25, 26, 27, 28, 29, 31, 32, 33, 39, 44, 45, 47, 49, 51, 52, 53, 54, 55, 64, back cover; Norman
Lenburg/FEMA: 5 (right); NASA: 10, 19, 30, 36, 37, 41 (infrared reading, left), 41 (bottom),
42 (image only), 46 (sidebar images), 70; NASA/Goddard MODIS Rapid Response Team: 17;
NASA Scientific Visualization Studio: 7 (right); NASA/Wallops: 15, 48; National Park Service:
16; Harold Pierce/SSAI/NASA: 20; Chad Rachman/Corbis: 3 (left); Radius Images, Corbis:
8-9; Brea Reeves/NASA: 23; Robert Simmon/NASA/NOAA GOES Project science team: 3
(right); Space Science and Engineering Center (SSEC), University of Wisconsin-Madison: 36;
Staten Island Advance/Ryan Lavis copyright 2016: 63; Tom Tschida/NASA: 40, 41 (top), 43;
UCAR: 38; United States Navy: 60; Marilyn Vasques/NASA: 33; Wikimedia Commons: 13

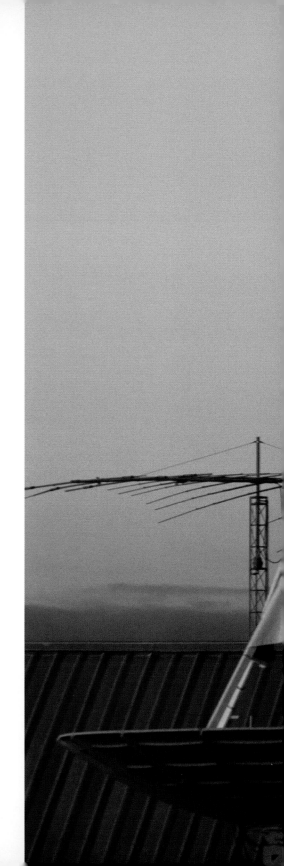

CONTENTS

1. SUPER STORM — 1

2. THE PHYSICS OF FORMATION — 8

3. A HURRICANE HUNT BEGINS — 15

4. SCIENCE IN A FISHBOWL — 26

5. UNDERSTANDING STORMS IN THE STRATOSPHERE — 35

6. HURRICANE EDOUARD AND THE SEARCH FOR THE HOLY GRAIL — 50

7. POLITICAL STORMS — 57

    Don't Be Scared. Get Prepared! — 65

    Glossary — 66

    Acknowledgments — 68

    Chapter Notes — 68

    Selected Bibliography — 70

    Index — 71

CHAPTER 1

SUPER STORM

On an overcast afternoon in late October 2012, thirteen-year-old Angela Dresch stepped onto the Staten Island beach that was a short walk from her home. Thick gray clouds boiled overhead as gusty winds whipped sea foam onto the sand. Halloween was just three days away and she was excited to go trick-or-treating.

It seemed strange that a hurricane was churning somewhere out in the Atlantic. Angela thought of hurricanes as summer storms. Coastal residents like the Dresch family accepted the risk of occasionally severe storms as a part of life, so Angela wasn't afraid of this hurricane. She was curious to see the angry-looking ocean, take a few pictures with her smartphone, and post them on social media. Maybe she would share them with her big sister, Jo Ann, who lived in Nashville, Tennessee.

Hurricane Sandy had been in the news for days, with weather forecasters calling it a "Frankenstorm," because it was almost Halloween. New York's governor had already declared a state of emergency. Some residents of low-lying coastal communities in New York and New Jersey were leaving their homes, but Angela's family decided to stay. The Dresches had evacuated during Hurricane Irene in 2011, and their house had been untouched by the storm. The unnecessary evacuation had been costly. While the Dresches were away, someone robbed them. They decided as a family that the next time there was a hurricane, they would shelter at home and protect their property.

The wind kicked up again. Angela was grateful for her favorite purple sweatshirt, which kept her warm. She pointed the smartphone at herself for one last picture, making sure to capture the gray skies and stormy ocean in the background. She smiled and snapped the photo. As she walked home to her parents, Patricia and George, she captioned the photo "#SANDYCOMEATME."

Angela takes a photo of herself the day Hurricane Sandy made landfall in Staten Island, New York.

By 6:28 p.m., the situation on Staten Island had deteriorated. Inside the Dresch home Angela sent a frantic text message to her friend Jenna Kelly.

"JENNA MY DINING ROOM IS FLOATING."

But Jenna couldn't possibly comprehend what was happening to Angela's house. In what looked like a scene from a disaster movie, a fourteen-foot ocean swell rolled into their neighborhood like a tidal wave. It was much worse than floating furniture. The whole dining room was being lifted from its foundation by rising water.

"George, get back!" Patricia shouted to her husband. In the time it took Angela's father to close the French doors behind him, the whole dining room was ripped off the house.

Hurricane Sandy had arrived.

Only a few minutes after Angela clicked Send on her text message to Jenna, the entire first floor was unsafe. The water was rising fast. The family knew they needed help. Patricia grabbed her cell phone and quickly dialed her brother's number. Gerard Spero answered and tried to reassure his sister. "I'm calling 9-1-1!" he said. Patricia hung up and prayed her brother would be able to send the police. But the lines were clogged with hundreds of incoming emergency calls. Gerard was placed on hold . . . for forty-five minutes.

Too late, the Dresches realized they should have evacuated when they had the chance. They were trapped. The only option was to move to the second floor. Photos and heirlooms tempted the family as they climbed the stairs, but there wasn't time to collect keepsakes.

George led his wife and daughter into the bedroom closet. They hoped they would be safe there, among the neat rows of clothes hanging around them. The floors groaned against the weight of water. The wind sounded like it could tear the house apart. Patricia touched the wall. Her hand came away wet and the plaster bubbled beneath her fingers. Water seeped in all around them. They needed to move again.

Angela followed Patricia and George as they raced into the bathroom. Maybe they could wait it out, holding on to the sturdy sink and solid bathtub. George and Patricia sandwiched their youngest daughter between them while the water continued to rise.

Before long, the bathroom was completely flooded. The Dresches were up to their necks in frigid seawater. It was getting harder to hold on to the slippery sink with cold fingers. Patricia gripped it with one hand and clung to Angela with the other. The water began to crest over their heads. They each took a big breath of air before they went under.

That's when the bathroom walls exploded.

The force of the collapse shoved the family out into what used to be their front yard. Now it was the ocean. One by one the family broke the water's surface, Patricia and Angela still holding hands. But something fell hard on their heads.

The roof.

They went under again. Beneath the black water, Patricia fought her way up, but something blocked her way to the surface. She reached out to push it away. Mother and daughter were wrenched apart.

Patricia resurfaced, gasping against the icy waves. She cast about desperately, looking for Angela, but saw only George's head above water. Where was their daughter? Both parents searched the punishing current for anything to hold on to. Patricia looked up and spotted a thick wire just overhead. She lunged and managed to grab hold, barely registering that her lifeline was a telephone cable, an estimated sixty feet (18 m) above the ground.

"Hold on!" George screamed as another wave overtook them. He disappeared, too. Patricia was alone and could barely keep hold of the cable. But she couldn't help her family if she went under. Looking around, she saw something familiar in the swirling water—her soap dish. It was still connected to the bathroom wall, which was floating next to her. Patricia released the cable and grasped the wall. She floated down the block alone on her makeshift raft and eventually made her way to shallow water. She dragged herself onto a neighboring back porch. Patricia had no idea what had happened to her husband or daughter. Battered, bleeding, and freezing, she drifted in and out of consciousness, praying

Angela and George somehow survived and that her family could be reunited.

When a first responder, a firefighter, finally reached Patricia, her body temperature was barely eighty-one degrees Fahrenheit (27 degrees Celsius). She was hypothermic and dangerously close to death. It was one a.m. She had been on the porch nearly six hours.

Patricia spent weeks in the hospital, but she survived. Tragically, Angela and George were among the fifty-three people in New York who lost their lives to Hurricane Sandy.

EYE-TO-EYE: HURRICANE SANDY

Meteorologists classified Hurricane Sandy as a "super storm," because a few days before making landfall, the weather system had collided with another large storm in the upper atmosphere over the Bahamas, greatly increasing Sandy's

size. However, the storm was still classified as a Category 1 hurricane, the lowest intensity on the Saffir-Simpson Scale, which rates hurricanes in terms of wind speed.

Many people, like the Dresches, falsely believed Hurricane Sandy's Category 1 status made it a weak and therefore less threatening storm. Sandy was not a weak hurricane. As it neared the Dresch home on Staten Island, it combined with a second system, an "extratropical" or winter storm, which provided a powerful burst of late-season cold air, making it a *hybrid* storm—a dangerous combination of multiple weather systems. By the time Sandy struck the East Coast on October 29, it was the largest Atlantic hurricane in U.S. history, with a record-breaking wind span of 1,100 miles (1,770 km) and peak winds nearing 115 miles per hour (185 kmph). Hurricane Sandy affected twenty-four states, including the entire Eastern Seaboard, from Florida to Maine, and as far west as Michigan and Wisconsin.

The Geostationary Operational Environmental Satellite System (GOES) imagery shows the East Coast engulfed by Hurricane Sandy's record-breaking size.

A makeshift memorial where the Dresch home once stood.

3

The boardwalk in Seaside Heights, New Jersey, sustained heavy damage during the storm.

Firefighters could only watch as an out-of-control blaze caused by Hurricane Sandy decimated the Breezy Point and Rockaway Beach communities of New York.

Sandy's size wasn't the only threat. One of the most destructive parts of a hurricane is its storm surge, an ocean flood on the mainland. These huge swells roll ashore when a hurricane makes landfall. And thanks to a full moon, the massive hybrid storm was riding an astronomical high tide. The storm surge was deeper because the tide was already at its highest point when the hurricane reached the coastline. Offshore buoys measured Sandy's highest waves at forty feet (12 m).

With so many factors contributing to its destructive capacity, Hurricane Sandy was no small threat—but its low Category 1 designation lulled thousands of people into a false sense of security. The hurricane decimated parts of New York. In New Jersey thirty-four people died and 346,000 homes were damaged or completely destroyed. Worldwide, 285 people were killed along the path of the storm in seven countries; 117 of them were in the United States. Though tragic, statistically those numbers are low. Wind

Sandy's mixed bag of weather dumped three feet of snow in parts of West Virginia, causing hazardous road conditions and large-scale power outages.

A fleet of New York City's iconic yellow taxis swamped by the storm.

and rain from hurricanes have claimed many more lives throughout history.

Torrential rainfall and heavy winds weren't the only havoc Sandy wreaked across the United States. The storm dumped thirty-six inches (91 cm) of snow in parts of West Virginia, crippling transportation and causing power outages to 8.5 million homes in twenty-one states. While Hurricane Sandy brought every phase of wet weather imaginable, it was fire that threatened New York's Breezy Point and Rockaway Beach communities in Queens. Just over twenty miles (32 km) from the Dresch home, Sandy's rising floodwater in these neighborhoods was a deadly soup of trash, jagged scraps of metal, toxic sewage—and fuel. Residents were trapped, surrounded by a contaminated, highly combustible flood. When salt water came in contact with exposed electrical wires, the flammable water ignited. Hurricane-force winds fanned the flames, burning over 150 homes and buildings to the ground. Firefighters were helpless because submerged roads made it impossible to access the out-of-control blaze.

A STORM IN THE CLOUD

Downed power and telephone lines all over New York prompted Hurricane Sandy survivors to use social media outlets like Facebook, Instagram, and Twitter to reach emergency services. The social media manager of New York City's fire department, Emily Rahimi, was at her desk when urgent requests for help began flooding the department's Twitter account. For thirty straight hours, Emily responded to hundreds of tweets, acting as a digital lifeline, relaying emergency requests to 911 dispatchers, and posting online updates about area flooding and fires.

Hurricane Sandy marked a technological shift in disaster survival. Social media platforms were used as a form of digital SOS, and in some cases, they were the only sources of important updates from government agencies trying to help injured and stranded citizens.

At the storm's peak, Instagram social network users uploaded Sandy-related photos at a rate of ten images every second.

The Red Cross monitored 2.5 million Sandy-related social media postings, tagging 4,500 of them for follow-up by officials.

In the storm's aftermath, social media remained a crucial component of disaster recovery until power and other utility services could be restored.

NYC Mayor's Office ✔
@NYCMayorsOffice

[Follow]

New Yorkers: Stay inside. Do not go outside. Being outside is incredibly dangerous. #Sandy

RETWEETS **567**   LIKES **32**

8:05AM - 29 Oct 2012

FEMA ✔
@fema

[Follow]

Phone lines may be congested during/after #Sandy. Let loved ones know you're OK by sending a text or updating your social networks.

RETWEETS **1,019**   LIKES **51**

5:29AM - 29 Oct 2012

The nickname "Frankenstorm" said it all. Sandy was a monster storm for the ages. Several years later, New York and New Jersey residents were continuing to struggle with rebuilding their communities, but it was even more difficult for them to rebuild their hope. Each year they worried that disaster might strike again. As terrible as Super Storm Sandy was, however, the loss of life and property could have been greater. Whether or not people chose to evacuate, they had time to prepare, because there were advance warnings. That hasn't always been the case. Before the advent of the telegraph, radio, modern satellite technology, and the Internet, some hurricanes made landfall with little or no warning at all.

Meteorology has come a long way since the turn of the last century. Thanks to weather satellites and early warning systems, today's forecasters can see a hurricane taking shape days—and sometimes weeks—before it makes landfall. Increased lead time means local weather bureaus are able to more accurately forecast the timing of a hurricane's arrival and notify residents if and when they need to evacuate. However, even with these new developments, too many questions remain unanswered and too many lives have been destroyed by these unstoppable storms.

Answering those questions has been challenging. Hurricane intensity is notoriously difficult to predict with great accuracy. Researchers at agencies like the National Oceanic and Atmospheric Administration (NOAA), the National Weather Service (NWS), and the National Center for Atmospheric Research (NCAR) are hard at work on the problem, studying the conditions under which hurricanes are created and where they begin. The first step to surviving hurricanes is to better understand them.

Sandy-related fires reduced neighborhoods to ashes.

The SUV-size TRMM satellite provided hurricane forecasters with 3D views of hurricanes such as Katrina in 2005.

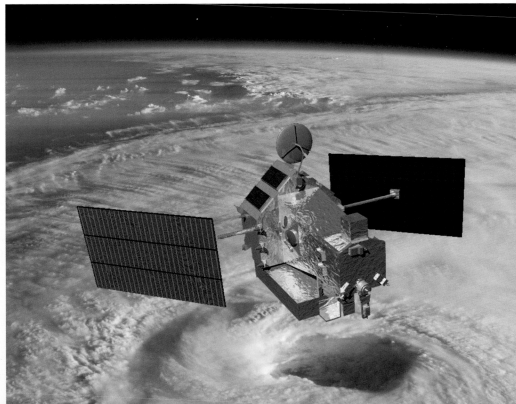

CHAPTER 2

THE PHYSICS OF FORMATION

Surviving hurricanes is about more than knowing when they will strike. These tropical systems can release the energy equivalent of ten thousand nuclear bombs and produce enough water to wash entire communities from the map. It's surprising, then, that these massive storms can begin in one of the driest places on earth. Most North Atlantic hurricanes are born amid the dunes of the vast Sahara as little more than a gasp of desert-choked air. The immense heat from the world's second-largest desert warms this tendril of air, causing it to rise above the

sand, where temperatures blaze near 120 degrees Fahrenheit (48 degrees Celsius). The searing newborn breeze curls onward, sometimes sweeping up grains of desert dust as it flows toward the coast, pulled by the moist air over the Atlantic Ocean. When this dry wave of energy meets moist ocean air, it collides with other storm activity already organized in the atmosphere. A tropical depression forms, which rises higher in a counterclockwise spiral caused by the earth's rotation, known as the Coriolis effect. Air pressure drops. Wind speed increases. Dense clouds darken the sky, producing wide rain bands, deafening thunder, and violent lightning. The hungry new system needs more fuel to survive— and there's a plentiful supply in the bathwater-warm ocean. The storm feeds, sucking heated water vapor inside itself, like a racecar engine stoked by gasoline.

The influx of additional energy causes the already low pressure at the center of the storm to plummet further. Winds intensify. Massive

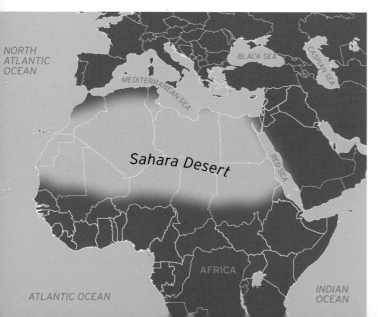

The vast Sahara Desert is a sea of sand that stretches 3.5 million square miles (approximately 9.1 million square km), covering one third of the African continent.

cloud towers launch fifty thousand feet (15.25 km) into the stratosphere, where temperatures are so cold it's actually snowing, while at the bottom of the system, immense heat and gale-force winds heave the ocean into fifty-foot (15 m) ship-swallowing peaks. The ferocious storm spools up *multiple* tornadoes and hurls cloud bands hundreds of miles away from its core, where the air is eerily tranquil. When Mother Nature's deadliest monster roars to life and its eye opens, nothing in its sight is safe. It's up to those in the storm's path to get out of harm's way.

That's the tricky part, though. Knowing when to evacuate people is the biggest challenge facing state, local, and federal emergency management officials before a storm hits. Timing is everything in a potential weather disaster. How much time is needed? How can anyone know for sure that an evacuation is necessary? If an evacuation is unwarranted, residents may be less likely to leave during future storms, and those consequences could be catastrophic. It's not enough to predict *when* a storm will happen. The future is predicting *how strong*.

Storm strength (intensity) determines how hurricanes are remembered throughout history.

Are clear skies ahead for stormy Jupiter? Astronomers at the Goddard Space Flight Center in Greenbelt, Maryland, report the Great Red Spot (the largest hurricane in our solar system) is shrinking. Recent Hubble Space Telescope observations confirm this storm is approximately 10,250 miles (16,496 km) across, less than half the size of previous observations that began in the 1930s.

Evolving tropical systems are given numerical designations until they reach a sustained wind speed of thirty-nine miles per hour (63 kmph), when they are classified as a tropical storm and assigned a proper name. Giving hurricanes proper names helps distinguish one storm from another throughout history.

The U.S. Weather Bureau began formally naming tropical storms and hurricanes in 1950. They started with the World War II military alphabet created by the U.S. military. Each letter was pronounced as a distinct word. "A" was Able, "B" was Baker, "C" was Charlie, and so forth. But every year the storm names repeated.

Today, the World Meteorological Organization maintains the list that is now composed of alternating male and female proper names. The list is reused every six years, but if a storm is particularly costly or deadly (like Hurricane Sandy), they retire the name and it can never be used again.

"Tropical cyclone" is the general term used for any hurricane, typhoon, cyclone, tropical storm, or tropical depression. Depending on where you are in the world, though, these storms are called different things. In the Northern Hemisphere, tropical cyclones of the Atlantic and northeast Pacific Oceans are called

hurricanes. They were named by ancient Central American civilizations that blamed the severe storms on the angry storm gods Hunraken and Huracan. Due to the earth's rotation, these storms rotate in a counterclockwise direction. In the Southern Hemisphere, tropical cyclones of the northwest Pacific are called typhoons. In the South Pacific and Indian Oceans, they are simply known as cyclones. In this hemisphere, storms rotate in a clockwise direction, because the earth's rotation pulls winds to the left. Down under, Australians have their own nickname for tropical cyclones: willy-willies.

It's always hurricane season somewhere on earth, but not even outer space is immune to cyclonic weather. The famous Great Red Spot on the surface of Jupiter is a hurricane bigger than our entire planet. It has raged for over three hundred years!

People cannot control the force of a hurricane, any more than we can prevent them from happening. The best thing we can do is better understand hurricane behavior and learn how to accurately interpret the ways in which they change and grow. It's a difficult task, because hurricanes are terrific secret keepers. But a team of elite scientists may have found a new way to see what hurricanes are hiding.

HURRICANE FAST FACTS

- Hurricanes are characterized by low-pressure centers. **The lower the pressure, the stronger the storm.**

- A hurricane does not have to be large to pose a threat. Imagine an ice skater spinning in a circle. When her arms are extended, she spins slowly. As she pulls her arms closer to her body, she spins faster. **The tighter and more organized the hurricane, the faster and more dangerous it becomes.**

- **Hurricane pressure is measured in millibars,** the standard unit of air-pressure measurement for meteorologists. It refers to how high the mercury rises in a barometer due to air pressure.

- **Hurricanes belong to a class of storms called tropical cyclones**. They vary in size, but are typically about three hundred miles (483 km) wide.

- A **hurricane watch** means that winds associated with cyclonic weather are *possible*.

- A **hurricane warning** announcement is more serious. It means winds associated with cyclonic weather are *expected*.

- **The right side of a hurricane is the most dangerous,** bringing storm-surge flooding, high winds, and tornadoes.

- **Hurricane-force winds extend anywhere from twenty-five miles (40 km) to hundreds of miles** from the center of a large hurricane.

- The winds around **the eye of a hurricane** are usually the **strongest.**

- In the past two hundred years, hurricanes have led to the deaths of nearly **two million people**.

- The National Hurricane Center uses the **Saffir-Simpson Hurricane Wind Scale** to give officials and the public an idea of what to expect from an approaching hurricane.

Anatomy of a
Hurricane

The term hurricane is derived from Huracan, a god of evil recognized by an ancient tribe from Central America. In other parts of the world, hurricanes are known by different names such as typhoons and cyclones

INFO GRAPHIC WORLD

■ LIFE CYCLE

Formation
Storms in disturbed area of ocean

Tropical depression
Thunderstorms start to swirl around a centre

Tropical storm
Winds over 39 mph

Hurricane
Winds over 74 mph

Saffir–Simpson scale
1. **Winds** 74-95 mph **Storm surge** 4-5 ft
2. **Winds** 96-110 mph **Surge** 6-8 ft
3. **Winds** 111-130 mph **Surge** 9-12 ft
4. **Winds** 131-155 mph **Surge** 13-18 ft
5. **Winds** 155 mph-plus **Surge** above 18 ft

Hurricane
Weakens after making landfall

■ INSIDE

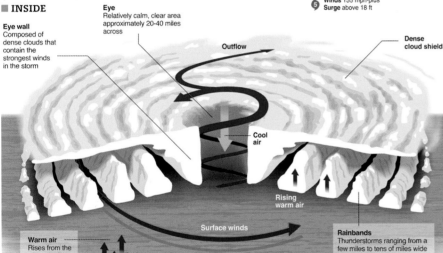

Eye wall
Composed of dense clouds that contain the strongest winds in the storm

Eye
Relatively calm, clear area approximately 20-40 miles across

Dense cloud shield

Outflow

Cool air

Rising warm air

Surface winds

Warm air
Rises from the ocean fueling the storm

Rainbands
Thunderstorms ranging from a few miles to tens of miles wide and 50 to 300 miles long

Infographics courtesy of NOAA, USGS, and Infographic World.

■ FORMATION

Hurricanes form over tropical waters in areas of high humidity, light winds, and warm sea surface temperatures (typically 80 degrees Fahrenheit or more)

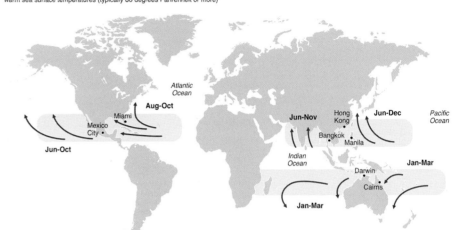

Atlantic Ocean
Aug-Oct
Miami
Mexico City
Jun-Oct
Jun-Nov
Hong Kong
Jun-Dec
Bangkok
Manila
Pacific Ocean
Indian Ocean
Darwin
Cairns
Jan-Mar
Jan-Mar

■ IN THE U.S. Landfall locations of major U.S. hurricanes 1900-2005

Category
3 4 5

Hurricanes making landfall in the U.S. by decade

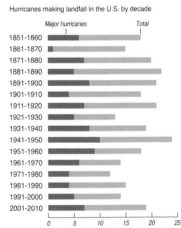

Major hurricanes   Total

1851-1860
1861-1870
1871-1880
1881-1890
1891-1900
1901-1910
1911-1920
1921-1930
1931-1940
1941-1950
1951-1960
1961-1970
1971-1980
1981-1990
1991-2000
2001-2010

0   5   10   15   20   25

HURRICANE INGREDIENTS: MOTHER NATURE'S RECIPE FOR DESTRUCTION

- Ocean water heated to 80 degrees Fahrenheit (26 degrees Celsius) to a depth of 150 feet (46 m)

- Moisture-rich air in the atmosphere

- Rotating winds over the surface of the ocean with little or no wind shear, a sudden change in wind speed or direction

- Thunderstorm activity

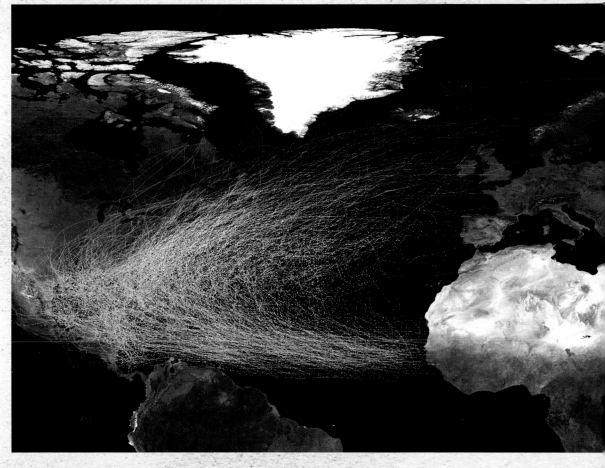

This map illustrates the tracks of all known Atlantic tropical cyclones from 1851-2012. The points show the locations of the storms at six-hour intervals.

CHAPTER 3

A HURRICANE HUNT BEGINS

Just a few miles down the road from Chincoteague Island and the pristine Assateague Island National Seashore is Wallops Island, home to the NASA Wallops Flight Facility. NASA may be best known for its off-planet projects like space shuttle flights, missions to Mars, and trips to the International Space Station, but the agency is also focused on more earthly concerns, like severe weather. In 2014, for the third consecutive summer, Wallops is hosting a world-class team of more than two hundred NASA engineers, meteorologists, and physicists, who have assembled here to conduct an airborne field science mission called Hurricane and Severe Storm Sentinel (HS3). Their goal: revolutionize the way hurricanes are forecast to make everyone safer.

CHINCOTEAGUE

Established in 1943, the Chincoteague National Wildlife Refuge covers fourteen thousand acres (57 km²) of beaches, sand dunes, marshland, and maritime forest. This diverse ecosystem is home to a herd of approximately 150 wild ponies and 320 species of birds, including bald eagles, great blue herons, and snowy egrets. Some of the island's birds are endangered, like the piping plover. These talented actors often pretend they have a broken wing to lure predators away from their young.

In 1965, Congress established the Assateague Island National Seashore, forty-eight thousand acres (194 km²) that encompass the Chincoteague refuge as well as the northern portion of Assateague Island.

A pair of piping plover chicks wait for their mother to return with a meal.

Two Chincoteague ponies accompany a foal to the shoreline.

Home to the NOAA Command and Data Acquisition Station, Wallops is the primary site for command and control of the United States' weather satellites. Meteorologists monitor the atmosphere around the clock as orbiting weather satellites ping crucial atmospheric data back to several large, white, dish-shaped ground antennas. Situated at varying positions across rolling acres of green pastureland, the dishes look surprisingly festive. Each one is outlined in tiny red lights that make it visible to aircraft. But these devices are the weather nerve center of the nation's forecasts.

Established in 1945 by NASA's predecessor agency, the National Advisory Committee for Aeronautics (NACA), the Wallops Flight Facility was constructed more than a decade before President John F. Kennedy challenged NASA to send a person to the moon. The 6,200-acre (25 km²) complex was originally built to conduct aeronautical research with rocket-propelled vehicles and is one of the oldest rocket launch sites in the world. When NASA was formed in 1958, components for the first human space flight program were developed here.

Today, the facility remains on the cutting edge of atmospheric research. Inside, the scientists of HS3 are using a special high-altitude unmanned aerial vehicle—a drone—to spy on Mother Nature herself in order to better understand hurricane intensity change in the Atlantic Ocean. Originally owned by the U.S. Air Force as a demonstration aircraft, this Global Hawk

On September 14, NASA's Terra satellite captured this image of Tropical Storm Edouard at 10:35 a.m. EDT.

drone now has a humanitarian mission, as a tool of science. For HS3 summer field campaigns, the aircraft carries a suite of onboard scientific instruments that allow NASA to study hurricanes in an unprecedented way—by flying over them for twenty-four hours at a time. If their high-altitude stakeout pays off, data collected by the mission could help rewrite the science of hurricane prediction. HS3 might save thousands of lives by helping meteorologists create more accurate hurricane intensity forecasts.

Scientists already know that hurricanes can behave dramatically within their surrounding environment at their uppermost levels. But

those places cannot be penetrated by traditional observation methods like radar and satellites. With this high-altitude drone, NASA scientists hope to collect data that will help reduce or eliminate unnecessary evacuations. They can be just as dangerous as hurricanes, because over time, repeated false alarms may frustrate citizens, making them less likely to evacuate during future storms. A more precise forecast could save untold numbers of lives and millions of dollars in unnecessary emergency management costs.

Luck hasn't been on the researchers' side during the three-year mission. The Atlantic hurricane seasons have been quiet, with the

exception of Hurricane Sandy, which, unfortunately, the team missed. By the time the historic storm had formed in the late autumn of 2012, the HS3 mission had concluded science flights for the season. Now it appears their luck might be changing. A tropical storm has organized in the North Atlantic and is forecast to strengthen within twenty-four hours.

Tropical Storm Edouard is expected to stay well out to sea and far away from populated areas. It's a perfect sample, and if all goes according to plan, Global Hawk could be there to record Tropical Storm Edouard transitioning into a full-blown hurricane.

At forty-four feet (13 m) long, with a wing-span of 116 feet (35 m) and a body that's two feet (60 cm) longer than a Boeing 737 jetliner at 112 feet (34 m), the delicate Global Hawk drone is the last aircraft any pilot would fly into volatile weather. But because it is able to cruise high above storms at nearly seventy thousand feet (21 km), Global Hawk can theoretically stay out of harm's way. And, since it flies autonomously, there's no risk to a human pilot.

Even though high-tech capabilities make the HS3 Global Hawk the ideal vehicle for the job, the use of drones is increasingly controversial. Other Global Hawk aircraft models are used in military missions, both as weapons and as spy planes. Despite the controversy, NASA remains confident that data collected during Global Hawk science flights has the potential to increase understanding of severe tropical weather systems worldwide.

The pressure is on for HS3 scientists. This is the third and final year of the mission's summer field science campaigns. They are running out of time, and some crucial pieces of data remain uncollected. Edouard could be their last chance to gather essential information to accomplish HS3's mission goals.

MISSION GOAL #1: UNLOCK THE SECRETS OF THE SAHARAN AIR LAYER

In North Atlantic hurricanes, the Saharan Air Layer (SAL) is an intensely dry, warm, and frequently dust-infused layer of the atmosphere that often covers the cooler, humid surface air of the Atlantic Ocean. Remember the Saharan desert dust that an emerging storm can pick up on its way to the ocean? This dust may be one of the large-scale *external* environmental factors impacting storm intensity. Does the presence of dust alter temperatures around the storm? If so, does it intensify or diminish storm energy? Some meteorologists believe the presence of Saharan dust makes storms stronger, while others argue it undermines the formation of hurricanes. This question is the subject of much debate within the meteorological community, and HS3 could help settle it once and for all.

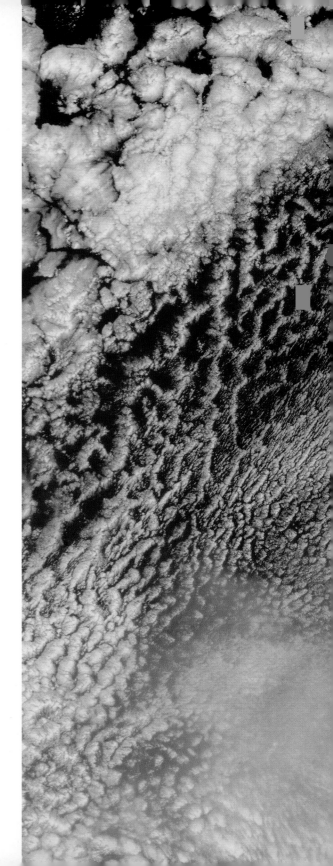

A large Saharan Air Layer
display captured by satellite.

MISSION GOAL #2: DECODE DEEP CONVECTION

Another intensification factor explored by HS3 is the role of deep convection towers. These immense columns of thunderstorms are *internal* to the hurricane's eyewall. The transfers of heat and energy that occur in this relatively small area

(roughly 10 to 15 percent of the storm's total surface) may drive hurricane intensification in the form of deep thunderstorm bursts within the hurricane's structure. But it's unclear what role these convective bursts actually play in the intensification process. What makes more of an impact on intensification: a bunch of smaller storms scattered throughout the system, or a smaller group of very intense storms? Scientists don't really know. These questions are hard to answer because hurricanes hide important clues about how they behave and intensify in areas that are hard to reach (and even harder to see). Some of the most powerful forces in a hurricane could actually be happening on a very small scale.

The HS3 team hopes their research will better explain a specific type of hurricane behavior known as rapid intensification, an increase in the maximum sustained winds of a tropical cyclone of at least thirty knots (56 kmph) in a twenty-four-hour period. (Wind speeds over water are expressed in knots, a unit of measurement equivalent to one nautical mile [1.9 km] per hour.) That's important to the ten million Americans who live within fifty miles of the Atlantic coastline. The speed at which a hurricane intensifies dramatically impacts how and when hurricane evacuations are issued. A more precise understanding of rapid intensification would increase the amount of time local governments have to get people out of harm's way.

Understanding how the combination of internal forces of deep convection and external factors like the SAL work to influence incremental changes in hurricane strength (and to what extent they can be predicted) could be the key to cracking the intensification code once and for all. And it all begins with a drone.

Positioning Global Hawk safely above Tropical Storm Edouard will require the skill of two highly trained drone pilots. But a third pilot is taking to the skies this morning as part of the HS3 mission.

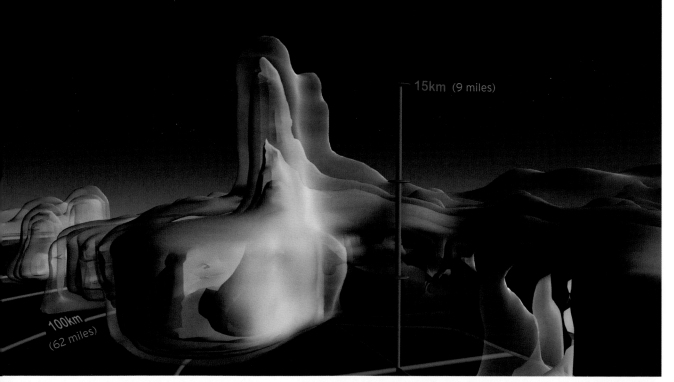

15km (9 miles)

100km (62 miles)

Infrared visualization of deep convection towers.

Dressed in a flight suit, his helmet in hand, NASA pilot Dennis Rieke inspects the shark-faced T-34 airplane that he will fly to escort Global Hawk while it safely navigates commercial airspace. (The Federal Aviation Administration, the national aviation authority of the United States, mandates that all drones must be accompanied out of commercial airspace by a traditionally piloted aircraft.)

Dennis, a recently retired Navy fighter pilot, has logged his fair share of intense hours in the cockpit. During his twenty-three-year military career, he flew jets in multiple combat zones over some of the world's most dangerous places.

His skills as a fighter pilot earned him a distinguished position as a flight instructor at the U.S. Navy's Fighter Weapons School, also known as Top Gun. "I got the chance to play the bad guy there," he says with a mischievous grin. "That was fun!" When he retired from the Navy, Dennis began flying with NASA.

FAA DRONE GUIDELINES

NASA is required to follow the guidelines of the Federal Aviation Administration. Strict rules govern the use of drones like Global Hawk in and around U.S. airspace.

- Must be accompanied out of commercial airspace by a traditionally piloted aircraft

- Must not operate in heavily populated areas

- Are forbidden to share commercial airspace with passenger jets

The NASA pilots Dennis Rieke and Gerrit Everson board their T-34.

Scott Braun listens carefully to the day's first weather briefing. Atmospheric predictions must be precise to protect Global Hawk from the dangers of high winds and lightning strikes.

After the exterior inspection of the T-34, Dennis and copilot Gerrit Everson climb into the cockpit and complete their preflight checklist. The canopy slides closed and Dennis cranks the engine. The tough little T-34 growls to life. They are ready to roll just as Global Hawk is towed into view at the far end of the runway.

"BOOM!" The explosion from an air cannon cracks the stillness. Global Hawk isn't the only large bird on the island. With the wildlife preserve nearby, the airfield is in the migration pattern of dozens of species of birds, some endangered. The Global Hawk may be the biggest bird on the block, at 25,600 pounds (11,612 kg), but a blue heron or bald eagle in an engine could spell disaster for the sophisticated drone. The air cannon scares them off, lessening the chances of injuring both a bird and the plane.

With the sky cleared of bird traffic, Global Hawk races down the sunlit runway. It lifts off, accompanied by the roar of Dennis's T-34 as it comes up alongside to escort the drone out to sea. When Global Hawk leaves commercial airspace, Dennis and Gerrit will return to Wallops, and Global Hawk will go it alone on a five-hour journey to meet Tropical Storm Edouard. As the two planes vanish into the horizon, the HS3 team far below prepares for the most important flight of the entire mission.

Global Hawk is a fully-automated aircraft, but it must be towed onto the runway with extreme care to protect both the plane and its onboard instruments. This is one of the last times human eyes see the plane for the next twenty-four hours.

8 A.M. WEATHER BRIEFING

With Global Hawk on its way to rendezvous with Tropical Storm Edouard, the scientists on the ground turn their attention to understanding the weather conditions it may face over the next twenty-four hours. Inside a conference room, the day's first weather briefing is about to begin. Leading the presentation is a group of early-career scientists who work with HS3 as part of their studies. The Pennsylvania State University PhD candidate Erin Munsell knows all eyes are on her. It's the first time the graduate student in atmospheric science has led the presentation. If Erin and the rest of the team are nervous, it doesn't show, despite the fact that they are charged with a big responsibility. For Global Hawk to successfully reach Edouard and record data, pilots and scientists must have a reliable forecast. Unanticipated weather conditions could compromise data collection and endanger Global Hawk, as well as its sensitive scientific instruments. Erin and her colleagues are about to share their forecast, which is designed to safeguard Global Hawk's overnight flight.

Erin Munsell and Christopher Melhauser, fellow Penn State PhD candidates, prepare to brief the HS3 meteorologists on Tropical Storm Edouard.

The lights dim as a dizzying array of maps, graphs, and complex charts begin trading places on-screen and Erin describes Tropical Storm Edouard's chances of becoming a hurricane. This isn't a "don't forget your umbrella" weather report. It's a forensic-level analysis of the atmosphere *by* weather experts, *for* weather experts.

Accurate hurricane modeling is an important tool in keeping the public safe from hurricanes. Forecasters rely on a worldwide network of supercomputers. These powerful computers use mathematical equations called algorithms to predict storm behavior. Meteorologists use this data to create storm models—or probable weather outcomes. The two most common are the American model and the European model. You may have heard them mentioned in your local weather forecast. While HS3 uses some of these models, their research requires a much clearer picture of storm evolution.

Erin, along with John Sears, an assistant researcher from the University of Wisconsin, and his colleague, Derrick Herndon, also a research specialist from the University of Wisconsin, helps create the hurricane models used by HS3.

"The models you hear about on the news have a fairly coarse resolution," Derrick says, "making it difficult to see what's happening in fine detail." That detail is crucial to an accurate HS3 forecast. "We have to run our models at a much higher resolution. With more data points crammed into less space, we can try to resolve the small-scale details of the storm. When we put the data from traditional global models into our higher-resolution hurricane model, we can use that data to create a better picture of what's going on." The whole team at Wallops—including Erin, John, and Derrick—is working tirelessly to do everything they can to ensure people

have the information they need in order to plan accordingly. Part of that includes getting the forecast right for HS3 so that Global Hawk can do its job.

Erin's summary continues. She explains how low wind shear will increase the storm's chances of becoming a hurricane over the next twenty-four hours. Wind shear is a sudden change in wind speed or direction over a relatively short distance. These abrupt changes can tear a hurricane apart. Without strong wind shear to slow it down, the storm can grow stronger and possibly undergo rapid intensification. The HS3 scientists at Wallops have never successfully observed rapid intensification during a science flight. With field campaigns concluding at the end of this hurricane season, Tropical Storm Edouard could be one of the last chances to capture rapid intensification, what the scientists refer to as the mission's "holy grail."

If Tropical Storm Edouard becomes a hurricane with the potential for longevity, HS3 might get another shot at it—and take an important step toward cracking the hurricane code.

As the morning weather briefing concludes, no one is certain what the next twenty-four hours will bring. One thing is perfectly clear, however. Tropical Storm Edouard will soon have a new name: *Hurricane* Edouard. Mother Nature is cooperating at last. Now the scientists must do their part. Every action must be meticulously executed from their high-tech laboratory on the ground: the Global Hawk Operations Center (GHOC), the scientific hub of the HS3 field campaign.

ARE YOU A FUTURE FORECASTER?

Do you chase rainbows? Delight in a downpour? Are you fascinated by the weather in all its forms? If so, you might be a meteorologist in the making. For this group of early-career scientists, there was never any doubt that the weather was in their professional forecast.

John Sears "I grew up in Florida. Once we had this serious hailstorm—like baseball-size! My dad ran outside with a sofa cushion to get some and then dumped them in the sink for me and yelled, 'Hey, John, look at this!' He knew I would love it. So I guess you could say I have always wanted to do science."

Erin Munsell "In 1993, Hurricane Emily was brushing the Outer Banks of North Carolina and there was a one percent chance it would hit the New Jersey shore where I lived. My dad let me stay up until midnight watching this crazy guy on the beach give updates. It was a hobby at first, but I always wanted to pursue it as a career."

Derrick Herndon "My father was very good at fostering my passion for the weather. We lived in Florida, and he gave me a personal weather-station kit when I was eleven. I used it to post my weather forecast on the refrigerator every day. I continued to use it for many, many years."

CHAPTER 4

SCIENCE IN A FISHBOWL

The Global Hawk Operations Center is filled with computers and high-tech electronics. As mission control for HS3, it consists of two separate but connected rooms, each one encased in glass. During a Global Hawk flight, the drone pilots and mission director are stationed in the "front room," and the HS3 mission scientists are stationed in the "back room." The team looks like they are in the world's most high-tech fishbowl—and the last place a person would want to be during a landfalling hurricane. Edouard will never reach the Virginia coast, but the team has a hurricane evacuation plan in place, should a dangerous storm occur.

The back room buzzes with activity, which could have something to do with how cold it is in here. The cooler temperatures prevent the computers from overheating, but make for chilly working conditions in GHOC. Some of the scientists wear fleece jackets to keep warm. All of these HS3 researchers are "on-station," seated at their computers, monitoring Global Hawk's five-hour flight to the storm. It's their job to make sure the aircraft and its payload devices are fully operational, while keeping a constant eye on the weather. Computer monitors flash between satellite and infrared images of Tropical Storm Edouard's telltale pinwheel formation.

The NASA research meteorologist and HS3 principal investigator Scott Braun at work in the "back room" of the GHOC.

Floor-to-ceiling windows separate the scientists and Global Hawk's large, stationary "cockpit."

A large flat-screen monitor on the wall broadcasts real-time video from Global Hawk's onboard camera as it soars high above the Atlantic. It looks like a video game come to life.

The two pilots flying Global Hawk are seated in the front room with the flight director. This is the aircraft's landlocked cockpit. All three wear headsets. Any communication from the front room to the back room about flight patterns or sudden weather changes must be relayed to the flight director first. Access to the front room is forbidden when Global Hawk is airborne. From the back room, it all looks deceptively simple. They could be doing their taxes with an ordinary home computer. It's hard to believe they are piloting a plane that is thousands of miles away using only a monitor, a keyboard, and a mouse.

From pilots and scientists to mechanics and engineers, the success of HS3 depends on how these skilled specialists come together as a team. Engineers work closely with physicists to build devices that collect storm measurements. Meteorologists look for shifts in the atmosphere that influence weather activity. The Wallops hangar crew keeps Global Hawk in good working order while it's on the ground, and the pilots keep it safe in the air. These storms demand this kind of diverse and detailed talent because they are highly complex and unpredictable. It's ironic that the career paths of some HS3 team members were as unpredictable as the hurricanes themselves.

Scott Braun, principal investigator for the HS3 mission, feels right at home in his enormous glass computer lab. The weather briefing was full of good news. He's hopeful about data collection for this flight, but the Wallops field campaign is only part of his job. As the mission's leader, he oversees HS3's many moving scientific parts before, during, and after data collection.

Although Scott has dedicated his life to understanding the worst weather in the world, this California native had no idea what he wanted to be when he grew up.

"To tell the truth," Scott says with a laugh, "I came out of high school not knowing what the heck I wanted to do. I can't say I was a weather geek. I took a lot of math and science classes but didn't connect that chemistry could lead to a career. I had taken an accounting class and thought, 'Hey, I can do this.' I chose accounting because it was the thing in high school that seemed most logical to me." So off he went to San Francisco State University to study accounting, proud to be the first person in his family to pursue a four-year college degree.

As a freshman, Scott needed one more class to complete his fall semester schedule. He arrived at the university's gymnasium to find hundreds of students in the same predicament. "The only table without a long line had two signs on it," he says. "One said GEOLOGY, the other one said METEOROLOGY. There was one person in the geology line and no one in the meteorology line, so I signed up for my first meteorology class."

Scott loved the course. "The professor was a real weather geek who spent spring break vacations chasing tornadoes in Oklahoma," he says. "I got infected by the same bug because he had so much enthusiasm in the classroom." But it would be one dark and particularly stormy night that first semester of college that would reinforce Scott's commitment to the science of storms.

"Growing up in Alameda, California, we only saw lightning on family vacations to Minnesota," he explains, and "lightning storms in the Bay Area are pretty rare. It was one a.m. and I watched an event that was constant cloud-to-ground lightning, something I had rarely seen . . . I was just amazed by it. That's where my interest in studying severe weather began."

Inspired by nature and eager to learn, Scott joined his charismatic tornado-chasing professor on trips to Oklahoma and California's Central Valley, hoping to spot funnel clouds and writing papers about them when he did. In graduate school at the University of Washington, Scott studied squall lines and flew into storms as an airborne storm chaser. "We had some fun landings, just trying to keep our lunch down!" he says, laughing.

After earning his PhD, Scott was hired by NASA's Goddard Space Flight Center in Greenbelt, Maryland. His work in hurricane research was as unplanned as his career in meteorology. "Goddard had an interest in someone doing hurricane work," Scott says. "So I began learning to understand them."

The weather briefing was full of good news, and Scott is optimistic about the potential for data collection.

Scott on-station in GHOC as Global Hawk gets closer to Tropical Storm Edouard.

Unlike Scott, Chris Naftel was captivated by NASA from the time he was small child. The soft-spoken southerner grew up regularly visiting the NASA Marshall Space Flight Center in Huntsville, Alabama, near his family's home. "I *loved* going to that museum," he says.

From the beginning, school aptitude tests pointed young Chris toward an engineering career, and after graduating from high school he was accepted into Auburn University to begin his studies. One afternoon, Chris went to learn about a new program allowing students to work and attend classes. He didn't know the meeting would change his life. "The head of the program was saying all the cool things you could do, like go work for NASA," Chris says. "A light went off in my head and I thought, *That's for me!*" Chris was accepted into the program, and at the age of eighteen he was already working for NASA, while studying to become an aeronautical engineer. That was the 1970s, and Chris has been with the agency ever since.

From his seat next to the two Global Hawk pilots in the front room, Chris serves as one of the HS3 flight directors. His job is to communicate with the payload manager in the back room to coordinate the position of Global Hawk with its pilots during HS3 science flights. But Chris is more than a flight director with HS3. In many ways, he is the reason the mission exists in the first place.

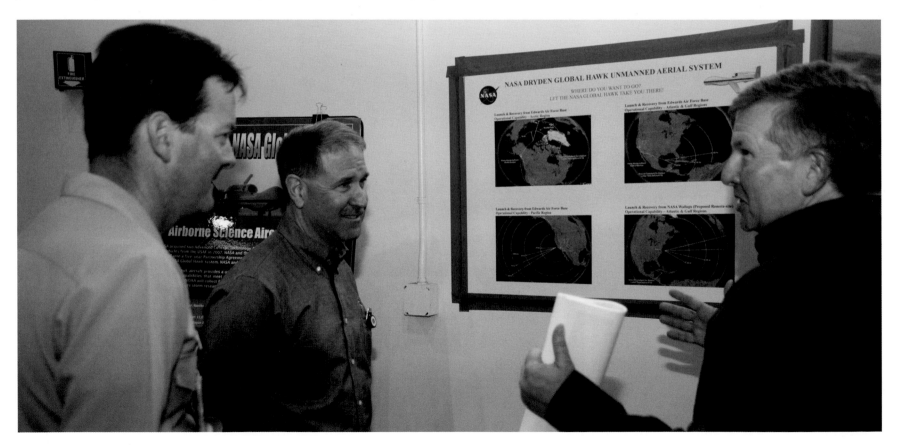

Chris Naftel (right) and the Global Hawk pilot Phil Hall (center) brief the former astronaut and NASA associate administrator John Grunsfeld (left) on Global Hawk's capabilities.

CHRIS NAFTEL'S BRAINSTORM

In 2004, Chris had just completed a NASA assignment and found himself in need of a new project. Having worked at the agency for so long, he knew the job was as much about creativity as it was engineering. He began learning about the Global Hawk aircraft, a high-flying drone that the U.S. Air Force was testing for military reconnaissance. He had this crazy idea that drones might be a new way to study storms. When he discovered the Air Force was finished with two of their Global Hawk demonstrator drones (used only for testing), the idea bloomed into his next project.

Since using Global Hawk to study the weather was Chris's idea, serving as a flight director is not his only job on HS3. Chris also works as a Global Hawk project manager. He is responsible for drone-related details such as creating schedules and reconciling the mission's budget. He also troubleshoots technical problems between Global Hawk and its payload systems.

"I'm your typical introvert engineer," he says. "I spent eighteen years sitting at a computer, then one day I'd had enough of that. I had to redefine myself." Chris went back to school with NASA to study project management. "Now I'm doing this!" he says excitedly. "Everyone comes to me with problems and I have to solve them, but not all of them are technical. People skills are a big part of the job." In some ways, Chris says, dealing with a high-tech drone is easier than dealing with the day-to-day operations of a complex science mission. "This is the hardest job I've ever had, but it's also the most rewarding."

Marilyn Vasques has also dedicated her professional life to NASA, running complex science experiments for the agency. Job satisfaction has always been at the heart of her career in science. She agrees with Chris that working on big field-science experiments is both challenging and rewarding. As an HS3 payload manager, she is the pipeline for all communication between the payload scientists in the back room and the flight director in the front room. Marilyn's role with HS3 requires a willingness to work with people and a knack for problem solving and planning.

Chris monitors Global Hawk's flight from the front room.

Seated at her station in GHOC, Marilyn quickly adjusts her headset and readies herself for the day's work. Like all other HS3 scientists, payload managers work overnight shifts on Global Hawk flights. "We make sure all of the principal investigators are in place for the engine start and we communicate with the flight director in the front room," she says. "We have someone on-station the whole time, taking turns throughout the night, and someone has to be here for landing."

Marilyn stepped onto her career path early in life as well: as her sixth-grade teacher's assistant. By the time she was a teenager, Marilyn had moved on to helping her high school science teacher create exams. "I was *always* the super nerd," she says, rolling her eyes. So when the high school principal called her out of class one day, shock gave way to delight when he announced that she had been accepted into a competitive NASA program for future scientists. One day per week, Marilyn would be allowed to skip school and work in a lab at the NASA Ames Research Center, forty miles (64 km) south of San Francisco.

Later, she returned to NASA. "I began working on experiments that were flying aboard the space shuttle *Challenger*," she says.

That all changed on January 28, 1986, when *Challenger* exploded, killing its entire seven-member crew. "When we lost *Challenger,* we

Marilyn Vasques takes the first shift of the day during the flight to Edouard.

were all devastated," Marilyn remembers. In the aftermath, Marilyn found herself out of a job. She had to pick herself up and find another one. NASA employees must be flexible and willing to work on different types of projects. Eventually Marilyn became a project scientist for STS-107: the space shuttle *Columbia* mission. Sadly, *Columbia* was another NASA shuttle disaster, exploding on February 1, 2003, as it reentered earth's atmosphere, killing seven more astronauts.

In the years that followed the shuttle disasters, NASA programs were streamlined or reduced. Marilyn began looking for work in NASA's Earth Science Division, which eventually led her to HS3. "I was managing animal experiments on the space shuttle," she says, "and meteorology experiments onboard an airplane isn't that different. It's all about teamwork."

Like Chris, Marilyn wears two hats on HS3, as both a payload manager and a project manager. Her deputy project manager is Bernadette Luna ("Bernie" to her friends). As with many of the other HS3 scientists, Bernie always excelled in math and science. She remembers her parents were big *National Geographic* fans, and when she was a kid, Bernie loved to watch nature videos about animals. No one was surprised when she decided to study bioengineering and later earned her PhD in mechanical engineering at Stanford University. "I actively look for things to fix," she says. "I'm not taking the toaster apart for fun, but if an appliance breaks, I search for information online and try to fix it myself."

Bernie's talent for engineering combined with Marilyn's background running experiments makes them a formidable team across many months of mission planning and preparation. Their work begins long before the other mission scientists arrive at Wallops. They tackle an impressive to-do list that covers everything from compiling phone numbers to coordinating drone flights through international airspace.

One of Bernie and Marilyn's biggest responsibilities is getting permission to fly Global Hawk through the airspace of other countries. The entire planet is divided into Flight Information Regions, and different countries manage those regions. Because Global Hawk flies over such large areas, Bernie and Marilyn work with the U.S. State Department to clear flights over forty countries. "It's a complex job," Bernie says, "requiring the ability to juggle many tasks at once."

While scientists like Marilyn and Bernie work to keep the project running smoothly, Chris and Scott ensure that equipment capabilities align with the mission's science goals. But there's another group of HS3 scientists who have a more specialized role with its own extreme challenge: their laboratory is seventy thousand feet (21 km) in the air and, at times, thousands of miles away from them.

Left to right: Marilyn, Bernie, and Scott on-station in GHOC.

Peter Black (foreground), a Naval Research Lab scientist, and Anthony Didlake (background), a research meteorologist at the Goddard Space Flight Center.

CHAPTER 5

UNDERSTANDING STORMS IN THE STRATOSPHERE

At its highest altitude, Global Hawk flies into the lower levels of the stratosphere. If this drone were a traditional airplane, the pilot would have to wear a pressure suit similar to an astronaut's.

You don't need a PhD in atmospheric science to understand that a hurricane is too big to fit under a microscope. So how can Scott and the HS3 crew use Global Hawk to survey and sample Tropical Storm Edouard? How can meteorologists possibly analyze a storm that is hundreds of miles wide and thousands of miles tall? That's the job of the three onboard

The earth's atmosphere is a thin sheet of air that encircles the planet, extending from its surface to outer space. It is sixty miles (97 km) thick and composed of five layers (troposphere, stratosphere, mesosphere, thermosphere, and exosphere). If the earth were a basketball, the atmosphere would be the equivalent of a thin sheet of plastic wrapped around it.

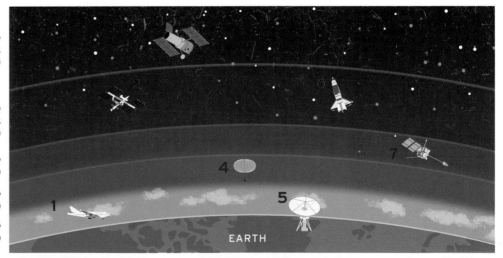

ATMOSPHERIC LAYER

Exosphere
373-6,214 miles
(600-10,000km)

Thermosphere
53-373 miles
(85-600km)

Mesosphere
31-373 miles (50-85km)

Stratosphere
10-31 miles (16-50km)

Troposphere
0-10 miles (0-16km)

EARTH

1 Boeing 747
2 International Space Station
3 Hubble space telescope

4 NASA super pressure balloon
5 Satellite antenna

6 Space Shuttle
7 Weather satellite

devices Global Hawk carries and the specialized scientists on the ground at Wallops, who will use them to spy on Edouard.

The physicist Gary Wick and the electrical engineer Terry Hock (rhymes with *joke*) are the dynamic duo behind the Advanced Vertical Atmospheric Profiling System, or AVAPS. Here at sea level on the Virginia coast, these two researchers are a long way from their Rocky Mountain home at the National Center for Atmospheric Research (NCAR) and the NOAA Earth System Research Laboratory (ESRL) in Boulder, Colorado. NASA is partnering with NCAR and NOAA to fly AVAPS aboard Global Hawk during all three of the mission's summer field campaigns at Wallops.

Both Gary and Terry point to an early longing to discover how the natural world works. Gary can't recall a time when he wasn't excited about

searching for answers. For Terry, it started as a childhood obsession with how the family television worked. You can hear the excitement in his voice when he recalls his earliest memory of wanting to become a scientist. "I was fascinated that we had all of these television shows, but I couldn't *see* or *feel* those waves!" The riddle of the television set sent him on a lifelong quest to understand what cannot be felt with human senses.

Working with the AVAPS device is ideal for

Gary Wick, AVAPS principal investigator, holds the dropsonde while his co-principal investigator, Terry Hock, holds its parachute.

Hank Revercomb is the principal investigator for the S-HIS device aboard Global Hawk.

The Cloud Physics Lidar principal investigator Matt McGill works with his team to install the CPL device on Global Hawk.

two scientists who live to ask questions and strive to reveal what is hidden in plain sight. Since Terry and Gary can't see their device when it's thousands of miles away aboard Global Hawk, their brand of scientific teamwork is a perfect fit for a mission like HS3.

Hank Revercomb has been working with climate and weather for forty years. "I enjoyed math and earth science in high school," he says, but like Scott Braun, he didn't begin to think about it as a career until college. After earning

his PhD in theoretical physics, he wanted a job that combined scientific theory with practical measurements, so he focused on weather and climate. From his office at the Space Science and Engineering Center (SSEC) at the University of Wisconsin, Hank studies the atmosphere by remote sensing (observing an object without making physical contact with it). During HS3 field campaigns at Wallops, he uses the remote sensing technology of a device called the Scanning High-Resolution Interferometer Sounder, or S-HIS, to scan storms from high altitudes.

Growing up in rural Michigan, Matthew McGill had a passion for two things: trains and problem solving. "I couldn't make a living playing with trains," he laughs. Matt knew he could make a living by using his skills with math and science, so he became the first person in his family to go to college. He eventually earned a PhD in atmospheric science from the University of Michigan. Now he works for NASA at the Goddard Space Flight Center in Greenbelt, Maryland. Using an instrument called the Cloud Physics Lidar (CPL) to study cloud structures inside hurricanes, Matt combines his love of physics and atmospheric science to help solve problems for people, like predicting severe weather.

GLOBAL HAWK'S POWERFUL PAYLOAD

The payload devices aboard Global Hawk, overseen by Gary, Terry, Hank, and Matt, are three strange-looking contraptions. One resembles a common vending machine, while the others could be alien creations from another planet. All of these devices are controlled from GHOC computer workstations via satellite uplink. The data collected from them could hold the secrets to understanding hurricane intensity.

Advanced Vertical Atmospheric Profiling System (AVAPS)
PRINCIPAL INVESTIGATORS:
Gary Wick, Terry Hock

AVAPS, or "the Coke machine," as it's known around the hangar, may resemble a vending machine, but instead of dropping drink cans, AVAPS dispenses dropsondes. Sometimes called sondes, these devices are powerful eleven-inch-

long (28 cm) atmospheric measuring tools made of stiff cardboard. They resemble the cardboard cylinder inside a roll of paper towels, but don't be fooled. These high-tech instruments are delicately engineered pieces of expensive scientific equipment. At roughly $800 per dropsonde, they'd be the priciest paper towel tubes on the planet!

How AVAPS works: Gary issues a remote LOAD command from a computer terminal at

Terry makes adjustments to the AVAPS device.

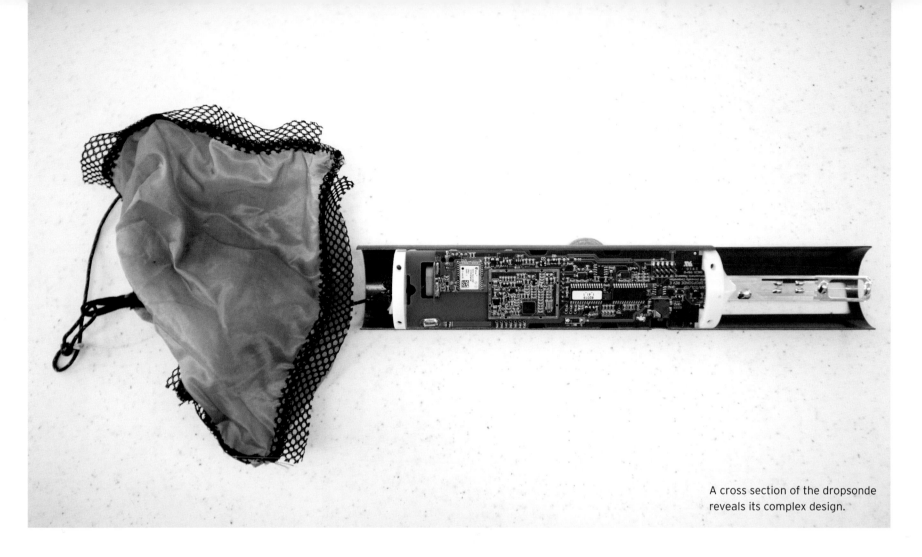

A cross section of the dropsonde reveals its complex design.

Wallops to AVAPS over the satellite communication system. Inside AVAPS, a dropsonde moves out of its rack, activates, and arrives in the metal launch tube. Within the launch tube, an infrared device—much like a TV remote—wakes up the dropsonde and initializes it for release. Meanwhile, back on the ground, Gary notifies the front room they are ready to launch. In the front room, the pilot checks for any air traffic below Global Hawk that might be impacted by a falling dropsonde. If the air is clear, the

go-ahead is given for the AVAPS team to *drop*. Then a second command is sent to AVAPS to *launch* the dropsonde. Finally, a plunger inside the AVAPS device pushes the dropsonde out the launch tube, and it falls into the storm. A small parachute releases from one end of the dropsonde, slowing its rate of descent. As it falls through the storm, it measures pressure, temperature, humidity, and wind speed. A global positioning computer chip inside the dropsonde transmits its position. By comparing transmitted

positions every few seconds, Gary can estimate how far the wind is moving the device to calculate wind speed and direction.

Because AVAPS data is reported from the interior of the storm to ground control at Wallops in near real time, this invaluable storm intelligence can be put to use by the HS3 team to determine Global Hawk's flight patterns. HS3 also shares dropsonde data with the National Hurricane Center in Miami, Florida. They use AVAPS data to fine-tune hurricane forecasts.

Stephen Crowell, a Global Hawk mechanic, mounts the dropsonde dispensing tube to the underside of the aircraft while Dave Costa of NOAA closely monitors the activity.

AVAPS can release up to eighty-eight dropsondes per flight. Their atmospheric readings are vital to the mission. If AVAPS isn't working properly, an entire science flight may be scrubbed.

Scanning High-Resolution Interferometer Sounder (S-HIS)
PRINCIPAL INVESTIGATOR: Hank Revercomb

How S-HIS works: From its position in the belly of Global Hawk, S-HIS oscillates, or swings back and forth, scanning over the storm structure in an area that covers about twenty-five miles (40 km). As it moves, S-HIS measures the thermal infrared energy radiated by the earth. By measuring the distribution of that energy, it's possible to determine temperature and water vapor profiles in the atmosphere. Temperature and water vapor create clouds which play an important part in energy conversion in a storm. Like AVAPS, S-HIS has both long- and short-term applications for the mission's research. In the short term, S-HIS data is immediately available via satellite downlink, so the information can also be used in real time to adjust Global Hawk's flight tracks over storms. In the long term, S-HIS observations of the Saharan Air Layer could help explain the relationship between storm intensity and desert dust.

Cloud Physics Lidar (CPL)
PRINCIPAL INVESTIGATOR: Matthew McGill

How CPL works: From its position near Global Hawk's nose, the CPL works by sending out five thousand rapid light pulses per second, which bounce and scatter off any particles they encounter. The light that bounces back to CPL can show how a storm's cloud structure is behaving and help determine the types of particles present in the atmosphere. Some of those particles are grains of dust from the Saharan Air Layer. CPL creates a better picture of the storm's anatomy to improve models of the Saharan Air Layer and expand understanding of how desert dust interacts with hurricanes. "We can see how high dust extends, how dense it is, and how much is there," Matt says. "Radar can't see that stuff because the particles are too small, but lidar can."

The Cloud Physics Lidar is autonomous, meaning it operates by itself. However, Matt and his team monitor it continuously throughout a flight. Like AVAPS and S-HIS, the device transmits data in real time, so its measurements are immediately available to scientists.

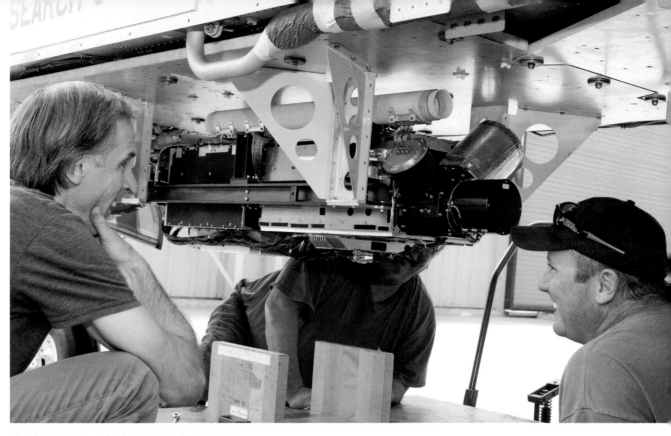
The S-HIS device is installed onto Global Hawk.

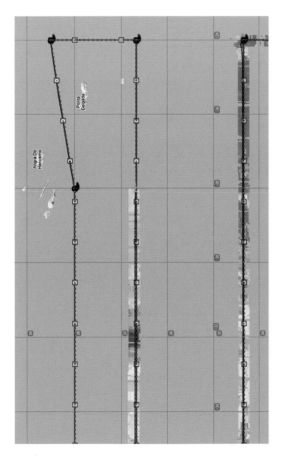
Infrared readings taken by S-HIS show colder temperatures near the center of a storm.

CPL and Global Hawk on the runway.

DRYDEN FLIGHT RESEARCH CENTER

BIG COMPLEXITY, BIG PROBLEMS

Global Hawk's large size and heavy payload capacity make it ideal for science missions. This diagram of Global Hawk shows the position of each payload device aboard.

Despite the sophistication of the HS3 mission's impressive aircraft and payload equipment, a big field campaign like this one is only as successful as the people who run it. With cool heads and a can-do attitude, they make "big science" look easy, when even the slightest change in weather or a minor equipment failure could compromise the mission. This team trusts each other to get the job done, no matter what happens. As Global Hawk zooms toward Tropical Storm Edouard, activity in GHOC is running like clockwork—quiet, organized, and efficient. It's hard to believe today's flight almost didn't happen.

"The problems started yesterday," Scott says. "We got in around seven a.m., thinking we were good to go. Then we found out the disk drive on the Cloud Physics Lidar device had not recorded any data for the previous flight. It wasn't clear if they could get it fixed in time, and we had a limited window to get repairs done and still be able to fly this morning." Timing is everything in a field campaign where so much can go wrong. Luckily, it was a relatively minor problem and quickly resolved, but that wasn't the only unexpected challenge the team faced.

They discovered the vital AVAPS dropsonde system had a broken thermostat. While they were able to replace it, they found another problem. "The release chute [on AVAPS] wasn't working, either," Scott says, "which could mean a jammed sonde at sixty-five thousand feet [20 km]." If that happened, the team might be without dropsonde data for the duration of the flight, a devastating loss given Tropical Storm Edouard's potential to strengthen. With the clock ticking, it was up to Gary and Terry's team to find a solution.

"AVAPS is essentially a two-button operation," Gary says. "You press a LOAD button, which moves the piece over and gets ready to start the initialization process. Then, like a Christmas tree, we see lights go on, telling us that the sonde is ready. That lights up a green button that one of us presses to launch, and AVAPS kicks it out. That's the way it works ninety-five percent of the time. But on this flight we had a problem."

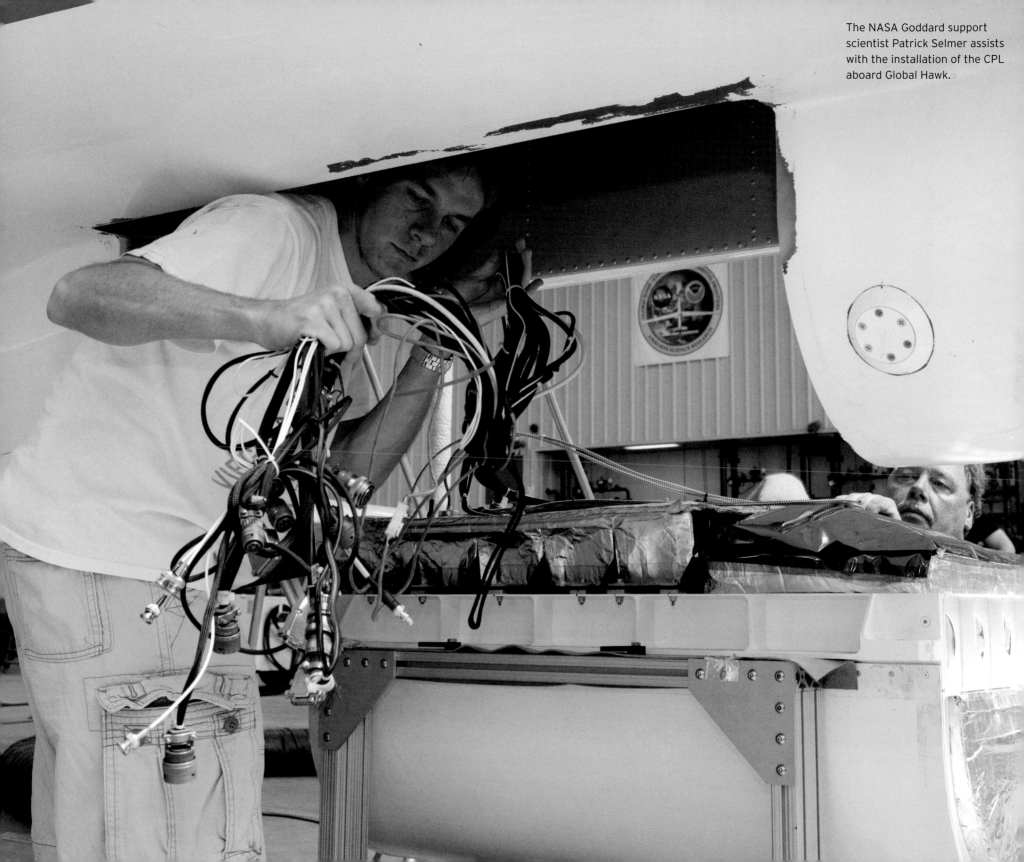

The NASA Goddard support scientist Patrick Selmer assists with the installation of the CPL aboard Global Hawk.

Stephen Crowell listens for flight status updates.

The team worked tirelessly throughout the day, but by three thirty p.m., the problem persisted. Meanwhile, the ground crew needed an answer, and one of the mission's best targets was spinning out in the Atlantic. It looked like Global Hawk might miss it.

In times like this, tenacity is just as important as technical skill for field scientists. By three forty-five p.m., Gary and the determined AVAPS team had devised a way to work around the problem, but the solution was not foolproof. For it to work, Gary would have to issue a *manual* command to release each dropsonde. It was risky, but without AVAPS, the team wouldn't be able to accurately measure storm intensity. Since Tropical Storm Edouard is forecast to intensify, they decided to go for it. Global Hawk would take off as planned.

It's a calculated risk, Scott admits. "If the positioning is not just right, they could still end up with a jammed sonde, and no way to release the remaining sondes housed inside AVAPS." Only time will tell if the AVAPS team's improvised solution will work during this critical flight.

GLOBAL HAWK REACHES EDOUARD

By early afternoon, Global Hawk has arrived at its target. Over the next fourteen hours, each of its three devices will gather data on Tropical Storm Edouard and, if the team is lucky, *Hurricane* Edouard. For now, everything is functioning properly. Matt reports that CPL shows no signs of trouble after yesterday's repair. As for AVAPS, the metronomic countdown of "three, two, one, release sonde" reassures everyone in GHOC that for now, the Coke machine is successfully deploying a dropsonde. Scott is pleased. "So far today, AVAPS has performed perfectly," he says. But there's a long night ahead and many more sondes to release. One by one, as many as eighty of the lightweight expendable devices will drop through the storm.

Field science isn't always as exciting as jammed chutes and last-minute malfunctions—it usually includes more mundane tasks like taking notes. During the course of an HS3 flight, Scott keeps a document open on his computer workstation. It is a daily science log, with collected images from the flight and summaries of what the team observes in those images. It includes details like what's happening at takeoff, what the team expects to see during the flight, and any unforeseen events that are part

of hurricane surveillance. Unforeseen events are the reason that HS3 meteorologists constantly monitor the weather, to make sure Global Hawk's flight plan safely positions the aircraft for data collection. GHOC scientists monitor the system's thunderstorm activity as well. If a large thunderstorm emerges on radar, Scott's team quickly notifies the flight director so pilots can divert the drone out of harm's way.

Global Hawk's flight plan must be filed with the FAA twenty-four hours in advance so all other air traffic can be cleared from the area. For tonight's mission, HS3 has requested a large three-hundred-nautical–mile (556 km) flight-pattern zone around the storm. The FAA will direct all other air traffic out of that circle. "We should be the only ones there," says Scott. "And that will make life a little easier."

LAWN MOWERS AND BUTTERFLIES

Global Hawk's flight patterns are planned in two basic shapes. Depending on the storm and what types of observations are being made, the aircraft passes over a storm in a lawn mower or a butterfly pattern. Sometimes both patterns are used during a single flight to maximize data collection.

Global Hawk's lawn mower flight pattern is characterized by straight lines and sharp turns.

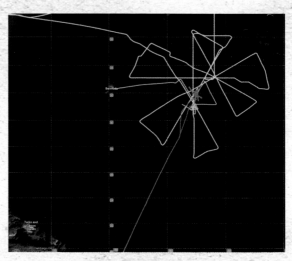

The butterfly flight pattern features long, looped passes over the storm.

Dennis Rieke reports for duty at NASA Wallops.

A DAY IN THE LIFE OF A DRONE PILOT

With only one drone to survey storms during this summer's field campaign, the pressure is on to keep Global Hawk out of harm's way during every flight. That's a job that rests squarely on the shoulders of NASA's drone pilots. Working inside the glass-enclosed chamber, wearing headsets, and dressed in traditional flight suits, the pilot and copilot sit side by side at their desktop computer workstations. Like the rest of the HS3 crew, they work eight- to ten-hour shifts during the flight.

NASA Global Hawk pilot Dennis Rieke explains that flying a drone feels nothing like flying a traditional aircraft. Drone pilots cannot hear the roar at engine start, see the ground below at liftoff, or feel the stomach-dropping sensation as it climbs. To Dennis, flying a drone feels more like office work.

"We sometimes joke that we are going to work in Excel for nine hours," he says with a laugh, referring to the popular spreadsheet software. "During a flight, we are working between multiple computer screens, using drop-down menus, pressing keys, and opening up program windows. It looks like we are just working on computers, but there is a real plane and it is flying off the coast of Africa at sixty thousand–plus feet [18 km]! It's seven or eight thousand miles away [12,265-12,787 km], and we're here in Virginia making it move with just a few keystrokes."

For a combat pilot who is accustomed to flying in hostile environments, the pace of the job can be a challenge. "When the drone leaves Wallops it flies in a straight line for many hours. There's really not much to do except monitor the system," he says. Dennis is quick to add that

there are other rewards of his job that make up for the lack of adrenaline. "The science is exciting. The ability to observe a storm by staying airborne for twenty-four hours is fascinating," he says. But it's personal, too. "The people I work with are enjoyable, and while I may not be defending the nation from the cockpit, I am still contributing to something larger than myself."

Despite how calmly these pilots carry out their work, there is always a chance something unexpected might happen. That's why drone pi-

lots rely on routine procedures that treat Global Hawk as if it's just another plane, like the T-34. Dennis says, "We have a pilot and copilot, and we do our checklists. The biggest difference is that we use a mouse and a keyboard to fly it."

Pilots must be on constant alert while Global Hawk is in the air. But some of the aircraft's best safety precautions are programmed right into its computers. "If the aircraft loses communication with us for a determinate amount of time, it will recognize that it is on its own and automatically execute a return to land here at Wallops," Dennis says. Like a giant homing pigeon, Global Hawk can always find its way back to the nest.

As the sun sets on what could be the most important flight of the mission, the day shift is drawing to a close for scientists, pilots, and technicians. The overnight crew yawns with coffee cups in hand as they enter the building. For them, the day is just beginning, as they prepare to settle in for a long night's work. Everyone is focused but cautiously optimistic. Will the AVAPS team continue to succeed in manually launching dropsondes without the dreaded jamming of the chute? Will CPL's repaired carriage continue working throughout the flight? And the biggest question of all: If Edouard rapidly intensifies, will it happen before Global Hawk runs out of fuel and has to return to Wallops? All that remains for the HS3 team is to work, wait, and hope.

Dennis pilots Global Hawk from the GHOC front room.

The NASA Wallops project manager Ron Walsh settles in for a long night.

CHAPTER 6

HURRICANE EDOUARD AND THE SEARCH FOR THE HOLY GRAIL

BULLETIN

HURRICANE EDOUARD ADVISORY

NUMBER 16

NWS NATIONAL HURRICANE CENTER

MIAMI FL AL062014

500 AM AST MON SEP 15 2014

AT 500 AM AST . . . 0900 UTC . . . THE CENTER OF HURRICANE EDOUARD WAS LOCATED NEAR LATITUDE 26.9 NORTH . . . LONGITUDE 54.5 WEST. EDOUARD IS MOVING TOWARD THE NORTHWEST NEAR 15 MPH . . . 24 KMPH . . . AND THIS GENERAL MOTION WITH A SLIGHT DECREASE IN FORWARD SPEED IS EXPECTED THROUGH TONIGHT. A TURN TOWARD THE NORTH IS FORECAST ON TUESDAY . . . FOLLOWED BY A TURN TOWARD THE NORTH-NORTHEAST TUESDAY NIGHT. MAXIMUM SUSTAINED WINDS HAVE INCREASED TO NEAR 105 MPH . . . 165 KMPH . . . WITH HIGHER GUSTS. SOME ADDITIONAL STRENGTHENING IS FORECAST DURING THE NEXT 48 HOURS . . .

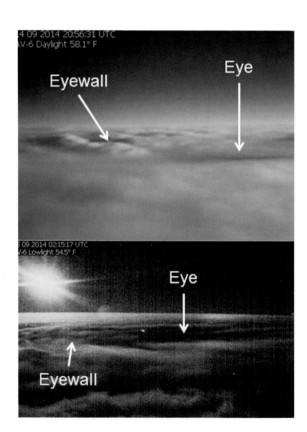

Two Global Hawk photos of Hurricane Edouard. The top image is a daylight view of Edouard's eye. The bottom image is a nighttime shot of the storm's eye illuminated by the moon, which is also visible.

Scales are rolled underneath Global Hawk so the aircraft can be weighed and its fuel consumption calculated.

Gary on-station during Global Hawk's flight to Edouard.

By seven a.m. the next morning, Global Hawk is on its way back to Wallops, loaded with good news. Overnight, Tropical Storm Edouard rapidly intensified from a tropical storm into a strong Category 2 hurricane. Rapid intensification was observed by HS3 at last, and the data was recorded. Scott explains, "According to my analysis, Edouard underwent a roughly twelve-hour period of rapid intensification followed by a short period of weakening as the originally very small eye was replaced by a much larger eye."

AVAPS worked like a charm. The capable Coke machine team dropped eighty sondes over the storm, and many were near the eye and eyewall. Gary is amazed after every flight. "You see the drone here in the hangar and it takes off and is on the other side of the Atlantic Ocean . . . it doesn't seem real—like something out of a movie."

Hollywood couldn't have written a better ending than this perfect flight during the last weeks of the mission. "Despite forecasts for a below-normal hurricane season, 2014 became our best deployment of the three-year mission," says Scott. But before they can download that data from the aircraft's payload devices, the drone has to be landed safely and returned to the hangar. A miscalculation at this stage would be devastating. No one can relax until Global Hawk's flight has concluded with a safe touch-down at Wallops.

To safeguard both Global Hawk and the data being carried onboard, its landing must be meticulously choreographed. "As the plane descends," explains Marilyn Vasques, "it makes a big drop at first. The air at lower altitudes will be warmer than at sixty thousand feet [18 km], and the sudden temperature change can cause condensation to form on AVAPS, S-HIS, and CPL. Moisture could damage the devices." As a preventive measure, instruments must be powered off twice during the descent to ensure that they're all dry and secure upon landing.

Minutes later, the T-34 and Global Hawk approach the runway. The smaller plane peels off, and the drone touches down on the tarmac in a whisper-soft textbook landing. With the sun glinting off its wings, it's hard to believe the drone has been operating at full speed since this time yesterday. The ground crew hitches Global Hawk to the tow vehicle that will return it to the hangar, where technicians must verify that nothing unexpected happened to the aircraft during flight. "That's always our plan," says

No one in the hangar rests easy until Global Hawk is safely on the ground.

Marilyn, with a sigh of relief. "No surprises!"

Inside the hangar Global Hawk is treated to a hero's welcome. Relieved HS3 scientists are buzzing, wearing big smiles and briefly trading enthusiastic handshakes. Hank Revercomb is pleased with last night's performance of the S-HIS device and hopeful about what they might discover from the flight. "We are learning a lot," he says. "It's exciting to see the process go from a concept to something you can demonstrate in instruments." For CPL principal investigator Matt McGill, these successful flights are about looking to the future of both the mission and the field of science. "In the past three years we did not get a lot of hurricane activity," he says. "But if we can help answer definitively whether the Saharan Air Layer helps or hurts hurricane intensity—it's a really great science outcome."

Hurricane Edouard shows no signs of dissipating in the next few days, and plans are already underway to deploy Global Hawk again. If the weather holds, it could be as early as tomorrow. As Scott leaves the hangar to attend the day's weather briefing, Global Hawk is fussed over by technicians and mechanics, who carefully weigh the aircraft to calculate fuel consumption. Eager payload scientists stand by to check the status of their instruments. The day-to-day duties of scientific progress are in motion once again. Now is not the time for analyzing the impact of last night's incredible achievement. That's a process that will take years.

Global Hawk touches down with the T-34 not far behind.

The conclusion of a large field campaign is just the beginning of scientific discovery. A scientist may spend years on the same problem, with little or no results. A successful scientist must be patient, curious, open-minded, and fiercely determined, no matter how long it takes to find answers.

The HS3 researchers know they have a long road ahead of them. They need time to sort through years of instrument data and get the opinions of other scientists in the meteorological community. Scott explains, "To study the data, synthesize what you're seeing, and combine it with other information—whether from satellites, other aircraft observations, or

other numerical models—piecing together the puzzle can take years. Then you have to write up your results. That can take another six months, depending on how fast you're writing." Field science is more than calculations and data collection outside the laboratory. Writing is another important scientific tool.

Scientists publish their research findings in professional publications called scholarly journals. When Scott's analysis of the data is complete, he will submit a paper explaining his findings to the *Bulletin of the American Meteorological Society.* Publications like these are an important way for researchers to share what they have learned with scientific colleagues all over

the world. Before results can be published as an article in one of these journals, they must be read, critiqued, and approved by other scientists in the same area of study. Once a scientist's peers have evaluated their work, it is published. "It can be a two- to three-year process from the time data is collected to publication," Scott says. "That's just the nature of doing science."

Analysis of the HS3 results is ongoing, but recent findings might be crystallizing the role of the Saharan Air Layer. Some scientists have argued that the SAL *directly* prohibits intensification, because when this hot, dry air enters the storm's inner core, it evaporates the humid air needed to create clouds. Since a storm's ability to intensify can depend on cloud formation within the inner core, the presence of Saharan desert dust could prevent intensification. However, early HS3 data suggests that the SAL's role might not be a *direct* influencer of hurricane intensity. "Right now our observations don't support a direct influence . . . but the SAL suggests an *indirect* influence, weakening the storm," Scott says. "We've often looked for the easy explanations. I think we're getting a better sense at what stage in the life cycle of a storm the SAL can play a role." Each possibility brings Scott and the HS3 scientists closer to solving the mystery of hurricane intensification and cracking the hurricane code.

A woman picks through the wreckage of her home in the isolated village of Myasein Kan in the Ayeyarwady delta, Myanmar, on May 20, 2008. It has been estimated that more than one hundred thousand people were killed by Cyclone Nargis. The storm left nearly a million people homeless in Myanmar.

CHAPTER 7

POLITICAL STORMS

What HS3 scientists learn during their patient and detailed study of hurricanes in the North Atlantic could make a difference for residents of the United States. It may likewise have implications for cyclonic systems in other world oceans—and the countries that are affected by them.

A better understanding of storm science is only half the battle. Hurricanes aren't just meteorological events. They can be social problems. How a city or government deals with the aftermath of a major hurricane can stand as a testament to its preparedness, or reveal shocking weaknesses in its ability to cope with natural disasters. Science alone cannot protect people. Local, state, and federal governments must be well prepared to act swiftly in order to keep citizens safe in a weather emergency. When government fails in the face of disasters like hurricanes, people die.

View of the aftermath of the massive Bhola cyclone and accompanying tidal wave (on November 12) showing villagers as they walk through a field of dead cattle and search for rice and other grains to salvage, near Sonapur, East Pakistan (later Bangladesh), late 1970.

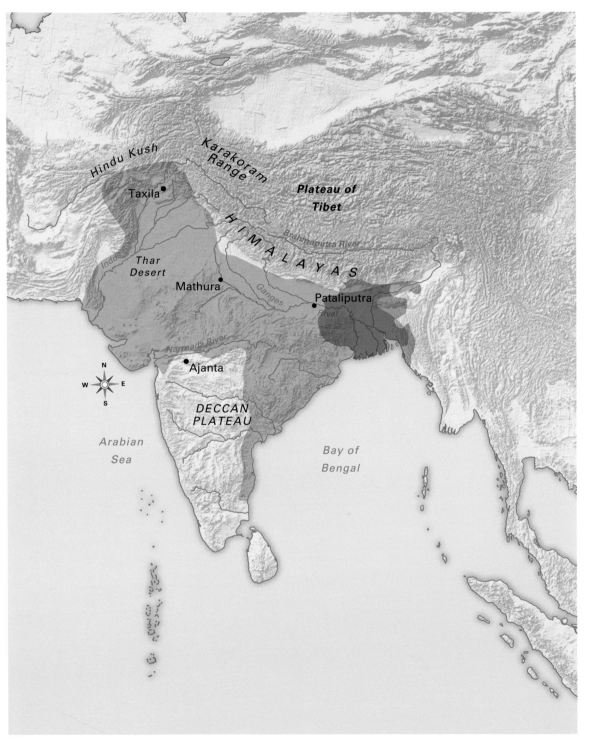

BHOLA CYCLONE

The area bordering the enormous Bay of Bengal (the world's largest bay) in the northeastern Indian Ocean is one of the poorest and most densely populated places on the planet. And from November to April each year, it is cyclone country.

On the night of November 12, 1970, while millions of farmers, fishermen, and their families slept peacefully in their beds or beneath the stars, the Bhola cyclone roared ashore in East Pakistan, a provincial state of Pakistan. No advance warning reached most of those who were killed, because communication was limited. Victims did not stand a chance against the 34.8-foot (11 m) storm surge, which meteorologists estimate was propelled by 140-mile-per-hour (225 kmph) winds, the equivalent of a Category 3 hurricane in the Atlantic.

The Bhola cyclone killed an estimated five hundred thousand women, men, and children. By the time the storm had passed, large numbers of bodies and livestock had been swept out to sea. Many more had not. Amid this unthinkable field of debris, desperate survivors fought to stay alive. They were thirsty, homeless, and

The area of the Bay of Bengal impacted by the cyclone, with the red indicating the hardest hit area.

An elderly man begs for food after the Bhola cyclone.

hungry, exposed to living conditions just as lethal as the storm itself. They ate tree bark, drank contaminated water, and waited for help that never came. Polluted water caused illnesses. Many more died. As survivors clung to life, the government scrambled to distribute food and fresh water, but insufficient disaster-relief preparation left it ill-equipped to help the large number of people in need. Ten days after the storm, most roads remained impassable. Racing currents made boat rescues and the distribution of lifesaving food supplies and medicine impossible. The area was paralyzed by the sheer magnitude of the devastation. East Pakistan had a humanitarian crisis on its hands. It would soon have a political crisis, too.

The instability of East Pakistan's government had been a concern before the storm. The government's failure to help so many desperate people after the cyclone hit fanned the flames of unrest. War broke out. By December 1971, barely more than a year after the storm, East Pakistan had become its own country, Bangladesh. A single storm has the power to divide countries and create nations.

HURRICANE KATRINA

A country's wealth is not necessarily an indicator of its ability to cope with natural disasters like hurricanes. In 2005, thirty-five years after the Bhola cyclone, the United States would face its own political storm. Hurricane Katrina was "the big one" that forecasters long feared would someday destroy the Gulf Coast region of the southern United States. Unlike victims of the Bhola cyclone, however, people in Katrina's path knew the storm was coming nearly a week before it hit. However, a mandatory evacuation of the city was not issued until the day before landfall. When Mayor Ray Nagin held a press conference the morning of August 28 and recommended the citywide evacuation, it was the first mandatory evacuation in the city's history.

That same morning, just hours before Hurricane Katrina made landfall, the National Weather Service in New Orleans, Louisiana, issued a chilling and plainly worded weather bulletin:

DEVASTATING DAMAGE EXPECTED . . . HURRICANE KATRINA . . . A MOST POWERFUL HURRICANE WITH UNPRECEDENTED STRENGTH . . . RIVALING THE INTENSITY OF HURRICANE CAMILLE OF 1969. MOST OF THE AREA WILL BE UNINHABITABLE FOR WEEKS . . . PERHAPS LONGER. AT LEAST ONE

Rising floodwaters threatened the entire downtown area of New Orleans, including the famed Louisiana Superdome. Thousands of displaced citizens sought shelter at the sports complex, before, during, and after Hurricane Katrina.

HALF OF WELL-CONSTRUCTED HOMES WILL HAVE ROOF AND WALL FAILURE. ALL GABLED ROOFS WILL FAIL . . . LEAVING THOSE HOMES SEVERELY DAMAGED OR DESTROYED . . . PERSONS . . . PETS . . . AND LIVESTOCK EXPOSED TO THE WINDS WILL FACE CERTAIN DEATH IF STRUCK . . . WATER SHORTAGES WILL MAKE HUMAN SUFFERING INCREDIBLE BY MODERN STANDARDS.

Many people chose to evacuate in advance, while thousands of others decided to stay and take their chances with the storm. For some, evacuating was a luxury they could not afford.

More than one-quarter of New Orleans residents (112,000 people) did not own cars and were dependent on public transportation. Among them were some of the city's poorest people, who lived in flood zones as much as six feet (1.8 m) below sea level. "Officials knew it was coming," said thirteen-year-old Antoine Williams, of the city's Sixth Ward neighborhood. "They should have gotten everybody out." But the city lacked enough vehicles to accommodate such large numbers of people.

On August 29, 2005, at 6:10 a.m. local time, Hurricane Katrina came ashore between Grand Isle, Louisiana, and the mouth of the Mississippi

River as a strong Category 3 system, packing 127-mile-per-hour (204 kmph) winds. The aging levees (embankments that protected the city from flooding) around New Orleans collapsed beneath Katrina's storm surge, which was over twenty feet (6 m) deep in some areas, flooding 80 percent of the historic city.

In the storm's aftermath, news coverage showed thousands of desperate people, some stranded on rooftops, and revealed deplorable conditions for the tens of thousands who had taken shelter in the city's sports complex, the Superdome. They begged for help, but local, state, and federal governments were slow to act. Completely overwhelmed by the scope of Katrina's destruction, the government's delayed response made things worse. Without food, fresh water, or medical assistance, some of the stranded victims died before they could be rescued.

Three more miserable days passed. People lost hope. Tensions rose. Frustration and anger combined with human suffering caused violent outbreaks among survivors forced to share close, uncomfortable quarters. Thieves looted businesses. Buildings were burned. Hungry people broke into grocery stores looking for food. Widespread relief did not begin arriving until five long days after the storm.

Many people asked how something like this could happen in the United States, one of the wealthiest countries in the world. In their report on the tragedy, the U.S. Congress concluded:

The response to the Katrina catastrophe revealed—all too often, and for far too long—confusion, delay, misdirection, inactivity, poor coordination, and lack of leadership at all levels of government . . . Hurricane Katrina found us—still—a nation unprepared for catastrophe.

Katrina caused more than $100 billion in damage. In Florida, Alabama, Georgia, Mississippi, and Louisiana, 1,833 people died. Of the 1,533 who perished in Louisiana, drowning caused 40 percent of the fatalities. Ninety thousand square miles (233,099 km^2) of the United States were affected, an area the size of the United Kingdom. Seventy percent of the occupied housing in the city of New Orleans was damaged. With nowhere to live, one million people were displaced, forced to relocate all over the United States as refugees in their own country. As of 2016, many of them had yet to return home.

THE GREAT DRONE DEBATE

No matter where hurricanes strike, they have the potential to become serious political and social problems. Scientists like those with HS3 are searching for answers, but the tools they use can also be political problems.

Some people believe the HS3 aircraft might carry powerful surveillance technology that could be misused to violate the privacy rights of people or entire countries. The HS3 Global Hawk drone never flew in combat missions for the U.S. military. It was designed strictly for demonstration purposes, not warfare. Other Global Hawk drones have been used for national defense, however. Is it ethical to employ drones as surveillance tools and weapons against other nations? As drone technology becomes more prevalent, and more advanced, these issues are of increasing concern, both in the United States and abroad.

Not every nation allows Global Hawk to pass through its airspace on its way to intercept a hurricane. In some cases, flying the HS3 Global Hawk through the skies of another country without permission could be seen as a serious act of military aggression. HS3 exercises extreme care when planning Global Hawk flight paths to respect the sovereignty of other world governments and their citizens.

New Orleans, August 31, 2005. A FEMA urban search and rescue task force helps a small child whose home was damaged by Hurricane Katrina.

Although NASA's use of the Global Hawk drone is as much a political decision as a scientific one, HS3 scientists and pilots share a deeply held belief that Global Hawk is an invaluable scientific tool. As Bernie Luna points out, "This is a project of global significance. Our planet is changing. There is potential to save human lives by understanding these storms better."

Time is of the essence. While no definitive link has been established between climate change and an increase in hurricane activity, melting polar ice caps could raise sea levels worldwide. Global warming could contribute to an increased flood risk during cyclones and hurricanes for heavily populated, low-lying coastal areas like the Bay of Bengal and the Gulf Coast of the United States. If humanity is going to continue to survive the hurricane cycle, scientists, local communities, and world governments must cooperate for the good of our planet and its people.

Scientists and lawmakers agree a better understanding of hurricanes will help save lives. But they can only do so much to keep us safe. With the tragic devastation left in the wake of storms like Hurricane Sandy, Hurricane Katrina, and the Bhola cyclone, it's clear that lives are at stake. We must be prepared, because year after year, people in the United States and around the world continue to face the worst of what the tropics have to offer.

Storms come. They cause devastation and loss. People suffer. They recover. And all too often, they forget.

REMEMBERING ANGELA

Every year on the anniversary of Hurricane Sandy, students and teachers at Totten Intermediate School celebrate Angela Dresch's life by wearing her favorite color, purple, to school. They come together to remember a young girl who was

funny, maintained a perfect attendance record, and had a big smile for everyone. The loss of Angela is a permanent reminder of a hurricane's power and the potential for destruction. Disaster can arrive unexpectedly and change lives forever, but we do not have to repeat the mistakes of the past. The harsh reality is that the hurricane cycle is inescapable. The good news is—it doesn't have to be hopeless.

There are practical things you can do to stay

Angela Dresch's friends celebrate her life with a candlelight vigil.

Scott Braun watches as Global Hawk disappears into the horizon.

safe and dry. Start with the suggestions on the next page. Stay alert for hurricane watches. Heed warnings when they come. Evacuate when necessary. Maybe you'll consider becoming a hurricane scientist.

In the meantime, the HS3 researchers at NASA are sifting through data for the raw material of discoveries that might impact the future of the hurricane forecast. With each passing year, scientists learn more about how to keep people safe before, during, and after hurricanes. One thing is certain. Meteorolo-gists like Scott Braun will be keeping one eye on the calendar and one on the North Atlantic. Hurricane season will be here before you know it. And somewhere out there, in a faraway African desert, a soft wind is just beginning to blow . . .

DON'T BE SCARED, GET PREPARED!

Hurricanes can be life-threatening weather events. With a little preparation and planning, however, your family and pets can stay safe and dry no matter what type of weather comes your way.

BEFORE THE STORM

Work with your family to create a disaster emergency kit with these items:

- Water—at least a three-day supply; one gallon per person per day
- Food—at least a three-day supply of nonperishable, easy-to-prepare food
- Flashlights
- Battery-powered or hand-crank radio that can receive NOAA Weather Radio broadcasts
- Extra batteries
- First-aid kit
- Medications—a seven-day supply—and medical items (hearing aids with extra batteries, glasses, contact lenses, syringes, canes)
- Multipurpose tool for minor repairs
- Tools/supplies for securing your home, like hammers and nails for boarding up windows
- Sanitation and personal hygiene items like toilet paper
- Copies of personal documents (medication list and relevant medical information, proof of address, deed/lease to home, passports, birth certificates, insurance policies)
- Cell phone with chargers
- Family and emergency contact information
- Extra cash
- Emergency blankets
- Map(s) of the area
- Baby supplies (bottles, formula, baby food, diapers)
- Extra sets of house and car keys
- Extra clothing, hats, and sturdy shoes
- Rain gear
- Insect repellent and sunscreen
- Camera for photos of possible damage
- A family emergency communications plan

PET PREPAREDNESS

Don't forget to create an action plan to care for family pets and other animals during hurricanes. Over six hundred thousand animals were killed or stranded due to Hurricane Katrina. Create an emergency supply kit for your furry family members. Keep your pets' important supplies (collar, leash, ID, food, medicine, carrier, bowl) in durable containers that can be easily accessed and carried. For more information, visit www.redcross.org/prepare/location/home-family/pets.

AFTER THE STORM

- Continue listening to NOAA Weather Radio or the local news for the latest updates.
- Stay alert for extended rainfall and subsequent flooding, even after the hurricane or tropical storm has ended.
- If you evacuated, return home only when officials say it is safe.
- Drive only if necessary and avoid flooded roads and washed-out bridges.
- Keep away from loose or dangling power lines and report them immediately to the power company.
- Stay out of any building that has water around it.
- Inspect your home for damage. Take pictures of damage, to both the building and its contents, for insurance purposes.
- Use flashlights in the dark. Do NOT use candles!
- Avoid drinking or preparing food with tap water until you are sure it's not contaminated.
- Check refrigerated food for spoilage. If in doubt, throw it out!
- Wear protective clothing and be cautious when cleaning up to avoid injury.
- Watch pets closely and keep them under your direct control.
- Use the telephone only for emergencies. Keep lines clear for others.
- If you smell gas, tell a grownup!

DIGITAL EMERGENCY RESOURCES

While it's best not to completely rely on Internet and digital resources (they may be unavailable if you lose power), there are many websites and apps designed to keep people safe before, during, and after severe weather events:

Federal Emergency Management Agency App
www.fema.gov/mobile-app

Weather Channel App
www.weather.com/apps

Hurricane by Red Cross App
www.redcross.org/mobile-apps/hurricane-app

First Aid by American Red Cross App
www.redcross.org/mobile-apps/first-aid-app

BOOKS

Looking for more information about these amazing storms? Here's a list of other books about hurricanes:

DK Eyewitness Books: Hurricane & Tornado, by Jack Challoner
Drowned City: Hurricane Katrina and New Orleans, by Don Brown
Hurricanes, by Seymour Simon
Inside Hurricanes, by Mary Kay Carson
The Superstorm Hurricane Sandy, by Josh Gregory
Weather, by Seymour Simon

GLOSSARY

Advanced Vertical Atmospheric Profiling System (AVAPS)—A device that launches dropsondes into storms from the Global Hawk aircraft.

Cloud Physics Lidar (CPL)—An airborne lidar system designed specifically for studying clouds and aerosols.

Cyclone—The term that describes a hurricane in the South Pacific and Indian Oceans.

Drone—An unmanned aerial vehicle.

Dropsonde—A weather device that is dropped out of an aircraft at specified altitudes and, due to the force of gravity, falls to the earth. During the descent, the dropsonde collects data about the surrounding atmosphere that can be remotely transmitted.

Eye—The low-pressure center of the storm's rotation, usually around twenty to forty miles (32 to 64 km) across. Here the winds are calm and skies are clear—even sunny!

Eyewall—The stadium-like cloud towers that surround the eye. Contains the strongest and most damaging winds and the heaviest rains. This is the deadliest part of the storm.

Hurricane—A tropical cyclone in the Atlantic, Caribbean Sea, Gulf of Mexico, or eastern Pacific, in which the maximum one-minute sustained surface winds are sixty-four knots (74 mph or 119 kmph) or greater.

Hurricane models—Mathematical equations that represent how atmospheric quantities such as temperature, wind speed and direction, and humidity will change.

Hurricane Warning—An announcement that sustained winds of sixty-four knots (74 mph or 119 kmph) or higher are *expected* somewhere within the specified area in association with a tropical, subtropical, or post-tropical cyclone. The warning is issued thirty-six hours in advance of the anticipated onset of tropical-storm-force winds.

Hurricane Watch—An announcement that sustained winds of sixty-four knots (74 mph or 119 kmph) or higher are *possible* within the specified area in association with a tropical, subtropical, or post-tropical cyclone. The watch is issued forty-eight hours in advance of the anticipated onset of tropical-storm-force winds.

Major hurricane—A hurricane that is classified as Category 3 or higher.

Meteorologist—A scientist who studies the atmosphere and its effects on the environment, predicts the weather, or investigates climate trends.

National Aeronautics and Space Administration (NASA)—The U.S. government agency responsible for the civilian space program as well as aeronautics and aerospace research.

National Center for Atmospheric Research (NCAR)—A research organization, established in 1960, that seeks to better understand our atmosphere and how weather and climate affect the earth.

National Hurricane Center (NHC)—The division of the National Weather Service responsible for tracking and predicting weather systems within the tropics of Central America and southern North America between the Prime Meridian and the 140th meridian west, poleward to the 30th parallel north in the northeast Pacific Ocean and the 31st parallel north in the North Atlantic Ocean.

National Oceanic and Atmospheric Administration (NOAA)—The federal agency focused on studying the condition of the oceans and the atmosphere.

Rain bands—Dense clouds that spiral around the eyewall and give the storm its telltale pinwheel appearance. They can span hundreds and, in the case of super storms, even thousands of miles.

Rapid intensification—An increase in the maximum sustained winds of a tropical cyclone of at least thirty knots (35 mph or 56 kmph) in a twenty-four-hour period.

Saffir-Simpson Hurricane Wind Scale—A one-to-five categorization based on a hurricane's intensity at an indicated time. The scale provides examples of the types of damage and impacts in the United States associated with winds of the indicated intensity.

Scanning High-Resolution Interferometer Sounder (S-HIS)—A device that measures emitted thermal radiation to gather information about temperature and water vapor in the atmosphere.

Storm surge—An ocean flood on the mainland caused by water from the ocean that is pushed toward the shore by storm winds.

Tropical cyclone—An intense circular storm that originates over warm tropical oceans and is characterized by low atmospheric pressure, high winds, and heavy rain.

Tropical depression—A tropical cyclone in which the maximum one-minute sustained surface wind is thirty-three knots (38 mph or 61 kmph) or less.

Tropical storm—A tropical cyclone in which the maximum sustained surface wind speed (using the U.S. one-minute average) ranges from thirty-four knots (39 mph or 63 kmph) to sixty-three knots (73 mph or 118 kmph).

Typhoon—A hurricane that forms in the northwest Pacific Ocean.

Willy-willy—Australian term for a severe tropical cyclone.

Wind shear—A sudden change in wind speed or direction over a relatively short distance.

World Meteorological Organization—A specialized agency of the United Nations. It serves as the body's authoritative voice on the state and behavior of the earth's atmosphere, its interaction with the oceans, the climate it produces, and the resulting distribution of water resources.

ACKNOWLEDGMENTS

I undertook this journey to understand hurricanes because I am no stranger to these storms. In 1990 I moved to Wilmington, North Carolina, a town in the heart of what's known as Hurricane Alley. Over the next ten years I survived the devastation of four strong hurricanes: Bertha (Category 2, 1996), Fran (Category 3, 1996), Bonnie (Category 2–3, 1998), and Floyd (Category 3, 1999). Then, during two separate weeks in 2004, the remnants of Hurricanes Frances (Category 2) and Ivan (Category 3) blasted the Blue Ridge Mountain counties (seven hours west of Wilmington), where my entire family still lived. Hurricane Frances flooded my grandmother's home with ten feet of water. Just nine days later, Hurricane Ivan followed a similar track and flooded the house again, this time to nearly eleven feet (3.6 m). But my family was safe. We know we were lucky. Families like the Dresches have suffered terrible losses to hurricanes.

Many people helped me write this book. First and foremost, I am grateful to Patricia Dresch for her willingness to share her story with me. I continue to be amazed by her grace, strength, and candor. I would also like to thank Scott Braun, Daniel Cecil, Gerrit Everson, Derrick Herndon, Gerald Heymsfield, Terry Hock, Keith Koehler, Bjorn Lambrigsten, Bernie Luna, Matthew McGill, Erin Munsell, Chris Naftel, Hank Revercomb, Dennis Rieke, John Sears, Joe Taylor, Marilyn Vasques, and Gary Wick. These generous people shared their time and expertise, both in person and by email or telephone. With an extended crew of over two hundred people, the HS3 team was too big for me to meet every member, but I thank them all for the important work they do. Thanks to Joe Lamberti for his revealing photographs! And to this book's earliest and fiercest supporters — my mom, Marty Cherrix, and pals Paula Yoo, Jessica Yodis, Cynthia Ritter, Kristin Jackson, and Ashleigh Tucker, thanks for believing. To Cynthia Platt, my good friend (and a very patient editor), as well as the whole amazing crew at HMH, I'm honored that you trusted me to tell this story.

CHAPTER NOTES

1. SUPER STORM

PAGE

2 *By 6:28 p.m.:* Rolando Pujol and James Ford, "Somber Funeral Turns into Heartrending Display of Support for Girl and Father Killed in Sandy Storm Surge," PIX11 News, November 13, 2012.

3 *fifty-three people in New York:* "Deaths Associated with Hurricane Sandy—October–November 2012," Morbidity and Mortality Weekly Report, CDC.gov, May 24, 2013.

3 *record-breaking wind span:* "Disaster Resiliency and Recovery Example Project: New Jersey and New York," National Renewable Energy Laboratory, May 3, 2016.

3 *Hurricane Sandy affected twenty-four states:* "Service Assessment: Hurricane/Post-Tropical Cyclone Sandy, October 22–29, 2012," U.S. Department of Commerce, NOAA/NWS, nws.noaa.gov. May 2013.

4 *Offshore buoys measured Sandy's highest:* Jesse Ferrell, "SuperStorm Sandy Stats: 95 MPH Wind, 40-Foot Waves," accuweather.com, October 30, 2012.

4   *In New Jersey thirty-four people:* "Deaths Associated with Hurricane Sandy—October–November 2012," Morbidity and Mortality Weekly Report, CDC.gov, May 24, 2013.

5   *The storm dumped:* Jesse Ferrell, "Hurricane Sandy Drops 3–5 Feet of Snow!," accuweather.com, October 31, 2012.

5   *"power outages to 8.5 million homes":* Federal Emergency Management Agency, "Hurricane Sandy: FEMA After-Action Report," FEMA.gov, July 1, 2013.

5   *Hurricane-force winds fanned the flames:* Andrew Siff, "LIPA, National Grid Sued for 120 Sandy-Burned Homes," NBC New York, July 3, 2013.

6   *The social media manager of New York City's Fire Department:* Yasmin Khorram, "As Sandy Pounded NYC, Fire Department Worker was a Twitter Lifeline," CNN.com, November 1, 2012.

6   *At the storm's peak, Instagram:* "Social Media: The New Face of Disaster Response" infographic, University of San Francisco Online Master of Public Administration Program. (onlinempadegree.usfa.edu/news-resources/infographics/social-media)

2. THE PHYSICS OF FORMATION

11   *In the past two hundred years:* "Hurricane Facts," conserve-energy-future.com.

13   *Hurricane Ingredients (sidebar):* NOAA, *Hurricane Basics,* May 1999. (www.HSDL.org/?view&did=34038)

3. A HURRICANE HUNT BEGINS

Unless otherwise noted, information in this chapter came from personal interviews with Scott Brown, Dennis Rieke, Erin Munsell, John Sears, and Derrick Herndon.

16   *Chincoteague* (sidebar): U.S. Fish and Wildlife Refuge, "Chincoteague National Wildlife Refuge" brochure, August 2007. (fws.gov/refuge/Chincoteague)

4. SCIENCE IN A FISHBOWL

33   *"It's a complex job":* "Meet Bernie Luna: Deputy Project Manager for HS3," NASA.gov, July 27, 2012.

5. UNDERSTANDING STORMS IN THE STRATOSPHERE

Information in this chapter came from personal interviews with Scott Brown, Gary Wick, Terry Hock, Hank Revercomb, Matthew McGill, and Dennis Rieke.

6. HURRICANE EDOUARD AND THE SEARCH FOR THE HOLY GRAIL

Unless otherwise noted, information in this chapter came from personal interviews with Scott Brown and Marilyn Vasquez.

50   *"HURRICANE EDOUARD ADVISORY NUMBER 16":* Hurricane Edouard Advisory Archive, nhc.noaa.gov, September 15, 2014.

52   *"According to my analysis":* Email correspondence with Scott Braun, December 1, 2015.

55   *"We've often looked for the easy explanations":* Agnieszka Gautier, "Profiles in Intensity: Unmanned Aircraft Probe the Secrets of Hurricanes," earthdata.nasa.gov.

7. POLITICAL STORMS

58   *The Bhola cyclone killed:* "1970 Great Bhola Cyclone," in "Hurricanes: Science and Society," hurricanescience.org.

60   *"DEVASTATING DAMAGE EXPECTED":* "Service Assessment: Hurricane Katrina, August 23–31, 2005," U.S. Department of Commerce, NOAA/NWS, nws.noaa.gov, June 2006.

60 *More than one-quarter of New Orleans residents:* Mary Gail Snyder, "It Didn't Begin With Katrina," Shelter Force Online, issue 143 (October/November 2005), nhi.org.

60 *"Officials knew it was coming":* Gavin Miller, *Hurricane Katrina Through the Eyes of the Children,* documentary film, 2012.

60 *On August 29, 2005:* "Hurricane Katrina Statistics Fast Facts," in "Hurricane Katrina: 10 Years Later," Cnn.com, August 24, 2015.

61 *flooding eighty percent:* Sarah Whitten, "Hurricane Katrina Then and Now in Pictures," cnbc.com, August, 30, 2015.

62 *"The response to the Katrina catastrophe":* Committee on Homeland Security and Government Affairs, *Hurricane Katrina: A Nation Still Unprepared,* S. Rept. 109-322, gpo.gov, 2005.

62 *Katrina caused more than $100 billion:* Ibid.

SELECTED BIBLIOGRAPHY

Belsey, Laura. *Katrina's Children.* Snag Films video. Shadow Pictures, 2008. www.snagfilms.com/films/title/katrinas_children.

Cline, Isaac. *Storms, Floods and Sunshine.* Gretna, LA: Pelican, 1943.

Larson, Erik. *Isaac's Storm: A Man, a Time, and the Deadliest Hurricane in History.* New York: Crown, 1999.

Miles, Kathryn. *Super Storm: Nine Days Inside Hurricane Sandy.* New York: Dutton, 2014.

Miller, Gavin. *Hurricane Katrina Through the Eyes of the Children.* Performed by Briea Stamps, Antoine Miller, et al. YouTube video, 50:07. Gavin Miller Productions & Ruston Junior High School, 2006. Posted by Gavin Miller, December 4, 2012. youtube.com.

Riley, Benjamin. *Disaster and Human History: Case Studies in Nature, Society, and Catastrophe.* Jefferson, NC: McFarland, 2009.

Sobel, Adam. *Storm Surge: Hurricane Sandy, Our Changing Climate, and Extreme Weather of the Past and Future.* New York: Harper Wave, 2014.

Some of the hard-working scientists and crew members of the 2014 HS3 summer field campaign.

INDEX

Bold page numbers refer to illustrations and their captions.

atmospheric layers of earth, **35**

AVAPS (Advanced Vertical Atmospheric Profiling System)

  malfunction, 42–44

  position on drone, **40**, **42**

  principal investigators, 36–37

  purpose and functioning of, **38**, 38–40, **39**

Bhola cyclone, East Pakistan (Bangladesh), **57**, **58**, 58–59, **59**

Black, Peter, **34**

Braun, Scott

  career path, 28–29

  on Edouard's rapid intensification to hurricane status, 52

  on equipment malfunctions, 42, 44, 45

  as HS3's principal investigator, **22**, **26**, 28, **29**, **33**, 45, **64**

publication of research findings, 55

on role of Saharan Air Layer, 55

on success of HS3 mission, 52

Chincoteague National Wildlife Refuge, 16, **16**, 22

climate change, 63

Costa, Dave, 40

CPL (Cloud Physics Lidar), 37, **37**, 40–41, **41**, **42**, **43**

Crowell, Stephen, **40**, **44**

cyclones

  benefit of HS3 research, 57

  Bhola cyclone, **57**, **58**, 58–59, **59**

  Cyclone Nargis, **56**

  regions affected, 11

deep convection towers, 20, **20**

Didlake, Anthony, **34**

Dresch, Angela, and family, **1**, 1–3, 63, **63**

East Pakistan (Bangladesh), Bhola cyclone in, **57**, **58**, 58–59, **59**

Edouard. *See* Tropical Storm Edouard

emergency management, 6, **6**, 10

evacuation

decision to ignore warnings, 1, 10, 17, 60

official notification to evacuate, 7, 10, 17, 20, 60

Everson, Gerrit, **22**, 22–23

forecasting of hurricanes. *See also* HS3 (Hurricane and Severe Storm Sentinel)

  agencies working to improve accuracy, 7

  modeling, 24

  by National Hurricane Center, 39, 50

  satellite monitoring, 7, **14**, 16, **35**

Geostationary Operational Environmental Satellite System (GOES), **3**

GHOC (Global Hawk Operations Center). *See also* HS3 (Hurricane and Severe Storm Sentinel)

  daily science log, 45

  flight director, **30**, 30–31, **31**

  front room and back room operations, 26, **27**

  morning weather briefing, **22**, 24

  payload/project manager, 31–33, **32**, **33**

  piloting of drone, **27**, 28, **28**, 47–48, **48**

  principal investigator for HS3 campaign, **22**, **26**, 28, **29**, **33**, 45

GHOC (Global Hawk Operations
  Center), *cont.*
satellite communication with drone
  equipment, 38, 40
teamwork, 28, 33, 37, 42, **70**
Global Hawk drone
altitude of flight, 35
AVAPS (Advanced Vertical Atmospheric
  Profiling System), **38**, 38–40, **39**,
  40, **42**, 42–44
CPL (Cloud Physics Lidar), 37, **37**, 40–
  41, **41**, **42**, **43**
deployment to Tropical Storm Edouard,
  17, 18, 23, 45, **50**, 53
dimensions, 18
equipment malfunction, 42–44
equipment payload, 35–36, 38, **42**, 52
escort through commercial airspace, **21**,
  21–22, **22**, 23, **54**
Federal Aviation Administration
  guidelines, 21, 22
flight plans and patterns, 45, **46**, 62
international flight clearance, 33, 62
landing, 52–53, **53**, **54**
liftoff, 22–23, **23**

measurement of fuel consumption, **51**, 53
piloting, 47–48
political concerns, 62
safety features, 48
S-HIS (Scanning High-Resolution
  Interferometer Sounder), 37, 40,
  41, **42**
use in HS3 summer field campaigns,
  16–17, 31
Global Hawk Operations Center. *See*
  GHOC (Global Hawk Operations
  Center)
GOES (Geostationary Operational
  Environmental Satellite System), **3**
Grunsfeld, John, **30**

Hall, Phil, **30**
Herndon, Derrick, 24, 25, **25**
Hock, Terry, **36**, 36–37, **38**
HS3 (Hurricane and Severe Storm Sentinel).
  See also GHOC (Global Hawk
  Operations Center); Global Hawk
  drone
analysis and publication of research
  findings, 55

base at Wallops Flight Facility, **14**, 15–16
findings on role of Saharan Air Layer, 55
global importance of research, 63
improvement in hurricane forecasting,
  15, 17, 64
mission goals, 15, 18–20
principal investigator, **22**, **26**, 28, **29**, **33**,
  45, **64**
summer field science campaigns, 15, 18
Hurricane Edouard. *See* Tropical Storm
  Edouard
Hurricane Katrina, 7, **60**, 60–62, **61**, **62**
hurricanes
facts about, 11, **12**
formation, 8–10, **12**, 13
glossary of terms, 66–67
on Jupiter, **10**, 11
modeling, 24
names, 10
preparedness and safety measures, 65–66
social and political consequences, 57–59,
  61–62
Hurricane Sandy, 1–7, **3**, **4**, **5**, **6**, **7**
hybrid storms, 3

intensity of storms
  external and internal factors influencing, 18–20
  numerical designations, 10
  rapid intensification, 20, 25
  Saffir-Simpson Hurricane Wind Scale, 3, 11, **12**

Jupiter's Giant Red Spot, **10**, 11

Luna, Bernadette "Bernie," 33, **33**, 63

McGill, Matthew, 37, **37**, 40–41, 53
Melhauser, Christopher, **24**
modeling of hurricanes, 24
Munsell, Erin, **24**, 24–25, **25**
Myanmar, Cyclone Nargis in, **56**

Naftel, Chris, **30**, 30–31, **31**
NASA Wallops Flight Facility, **14**, 15–16. *See also* HS3 (Hurricane and Severe Storm Sentinel)
National Center for Atmospheric Research (NCAR), 7, 36
National Hurricane Center (NHC), 39, 50

National Oceanic and Atmospheric Administration (NOAA), 7, 16, 36, **40**
National Weather Service (NWS), 7, 60
New Orleans, Hurricane Katrina in, **7**, **60**, 60–62, **61**, **62**
New York and New Jersey, Hurricane Sandy in, 1–7, **3**, **4**, **5**, **6**, 7

preparedness, 65–66

Rahimi, Emily, 6, **6**
rapid intensification, 20, 25
Revercomb, Hank, **36**, 37, 53
Rieke, Dennis, 21–23, **22**, **47**, 47–48

safety measures, 65–66
Saffir-Simpson Hurricane Wind Scale, 3, 11, **12**
Sahara Desert, 8–10, **9**
SAL (Saharan Air Layer), 18, **19**, 40–41, 55
satellite tracking, **3**, **7**, **14**, 16, **17**, **19**
Scanning High-Resolution Interferometer Sounder (S-HIS), 37, 40, **41**, **42**
Sears, John, 24, 25, **25**

Selmer, Patrick, **43**
S-HIS (Scanning High-Resolution Interferometer Sounder), 37, 40, **41**, **42**
social media, 6
strength of storms. *See* intensity of storms

tropical cyclones, 10–11, **13**
Tropical Storm Edouard
  collection of data about, 17, 18, 25, 45, **50**, 53
  rapid intensification to hurricane status, 25, 50, 52
  satellite image of, **17**
typhoons, 11

Vasques, Marilyn, 31–33, **32**, **33**, 52–53

Wallops Flight Facility, **14**, 15–16. *See also* HS3 (Hurricane and Severe Storm Sentinel)
Walsh, Ron, **49**
Wick, Gary, **36**, 36–37, 44, **52**
wind shear, 25
wind speed. *See* intensity of storms

SCIENTISTS IN THE FIELD
WHERE SCIENCE MEETS ADVENTURE

Check out these titles to meet more scientists who are out in the field—and contributing every day to our knowledge of the world around us:

Looking for even more adventure? Craving updates on the work of your favorite scientists, as well as in-depth video footage, audio, photography, and more? Then visit the new Scientists in the Field website!

WWW.SCIENCEMEETSADVENTURE.COM